COMPREHENSIVE PROSPERITY

"Prosperity refers to a state of thriving, abundance, and success in various aspects of life, such as financial wealth, personal well-being, social progress, and overall flourishing. It implies the presence of favorable circumstances, opportunities for growth, and the attainment of goals, leading to a high standard of living and overall satisfaction."

Praise for *The Prosperous Veterinarian*

"*The Prosperous Veterinarian* is a must read for any veterinarian who wants to become more effective in their personal and professional life. I have known Andy for many years and have a great deal of confidence and respect for his knowledge of both money management and veterinary medicine. Andy has always been very generous in sharing his experience and knowledge with the veterinary community. This book is a selfless sharing of essential knowledge in personal and business-related financial management; fields that few veterinarians master. If one reads this book and follows the principles of wealth building that Andy et al. explain, you will prosper in an ethical and unselfish way. I commend Andy on presenting an important topic and explaining it in an understandable fashion as only he can do. Thanks to the authors for a book that has been long needed in veterinary medicine!"

John Payne DVM, MS, DACVS

"*The Prosperous Veterinarian* delivers invaluable advice for veterinarians aiming for success, both financially and personally. The contributors' stories are engaging and full of practical wisdom, making the book a powerful resource. The book's clear guidance and well-chosen resources set veterinarians on a path to a prosperous and fulfilling career."

Julie D. Smith, DVM, DACVS, CCRT, MBA

"The insights and guidance in *The Prosperous Veterinarian* are invaluable. As a veterinarian and entrepreneur who initially struggled with a guilt-tinged point of view on our profession's relationship with money—sadly reinforced by bullying from clients and even my own colleagues—I found this book to offer a fresh and empowering perspective on financial prosperity, providing practical strategies that resonate with our unique profession. It's a must-read for any veterinarian seeking to build a fulfilling and financially secure career."

Cindy Trice, DVM; CVO, Hound; founder, Relief Rover, Relief Veterinarian; and founder, Kickit Pajamas

"Many of us feel guilty about our success. After reading this book, we should all recognize that being a good, caring, compassionate veterinarian can be very rewarding emotionally and financially. And understanding how to handle that financial prosperity when done correctly will set you up for a lifetime of achievement, happiness, and success without apology. If you are looking for a roadmap to help get you from where you are to where you need to be, start here."

Peter Weinstein, DVM, MBA; co-author, *The E-Myth Veterinarian: Why Most Veterinary Practices Don't Work and What to Do About It*; president, PAW Consulting

"In a world that rarely seems straightforward, *The Prosperous Veterinarian*, is a sincere and honest examination of the obstacles that hold back many veterinarians. If you're looking for a way to take back your life, both personally and professionally, look no further. This book gives you the tools and encouragement needed to make real changes in your trajectory. Grab a pen, highlighter, and a cup of coffee, and jump in."

Nichole D'Intino, DVM; partner, CityVet—Alamo Heights

"Rather than being a goal, money is a tool. It makes sense to know how to best use it. It makes sense to take care of it. It makes sense to understand it. We should all be on the journey to prosperity, and Andy Anderson's *The Prosperous Veterinarian* presents a guide worth following."

Andy Bailey, founder, www.Boundless.me; founder, Petra Coaching; author, *No Try, Only Do* and *Vitamin B (For Business)*

THE
PROSPEROUS
VETERINARIAN

THE
PROSPEROUS
VETERINARIAN

How to Take Control of Your Life and Transform Our Profession

ANDY ANDERSON DVM MBA

WITH CONTRIBUTIONS FROM
Jennifer Welser, DVM Chip Cannon, DVM Brent Mayabb, DVM

First edition September, 2024

Copyright © Andy Anderson, 2024

All rights reserved. No part of this book may be reproduced, distributed, or transmitted in any form or by any means, including photocopying, recording, or other electronic or mechanical methods, without the prior written permission of the author, except for the use of quotations in a book review. For permission requests: info@theprosperousvet.com

Although every precaution has been taken to verify the accuracy of the information contained herein, the author assumes no responsibility for any errors or omissions. No liability is assumed for losses or damages that may result from the use of information contained within. You are responsible for your own choices, actions, and results.

ISBN: 979-8-9915030-0-6 (hardcover dustjacket)
ISBN: 979-8-9915030-1-3 (ebook)

Book design by G Sharp Design, LLC

To my mentors, whose unselfish sharing of knowledge
lit my path and sustained me.

CONTENTS

Foreword xiii

Preface. xix

Chapter 1   The Veterinary Degree as an Engine of
            Prosperity. 1

Chapter 2   The Veterinarian's Dysfunctional
            Relationship with Money 19

Chapter 3   What is Prosperity, Anyway? 41

Chapter 4   The Principles of Money. 59

Chapter 5   Three Predictable Paths to Financial
            Prosperity. 79

Chapter 6   The Five Stages of the Financially
            Prosperous Veterinarian 113

Chapter 7   Building Cash Flow through the Hybrid
            Ownership Model 131

Chapter 8   On Entrepreneurship, Mentorship, and
            Association 145

Chapter 9   Practical Truths for Life 165

Chapter 10 A Life Operating System 179

Conclusion. 199

Acknowledgments 207

About the Author 209

FOREWORD

Rustin M. Moore, DVM, PhD, Diplomate ACVS
Dean, The Ohio State University College of Veterinary Medicine
President, American Association of Veterinary Medical Colleges
Author, *UNLEASHING THE BOND: Harnessing the Benefits and Safeguarding the Risks of Human-Animal Interactions*

In a world where the noble calling of veterinary medicine often intersects with the harsh realities of financial pressures and corporate cultures, here emerges a voice of clarity and purpose—one that transcends the conventional boundaries of our beloved veterinary profession.

Author Andy Anderson, DVM, has dedicated over two decades to a mission that many of us only dream of undertaking, to bridge the gap between clinical expertise and financial prosperity, and to guide us toward a future where both are not just achievable, but harmonious.

As a colleague who has witnessed firsthand the struggles and triumphs of veterinarians, I can attest to the transformative power of the principles shared within these pages. Dr.

Anderson's journey is not just one of personal success but of a deep commitment to uplifting our entire profession.

Through countless conversations, investments, and mentoring experiences, Dr. Anderson and the contributing authors have distilled the wisdom of many into a practical guide that speaks to our shared purpose—our capital-P Purpose—of serving animals and people.

The notion that veterinary medicine is a powerful economic asset is not new, but the approach to unlocking its potential, as laid out in this book, is both refreshing and necessary. The emphasis on personal responsibility, non-financial prosperity, and the development of a Life Operating System is a testament to Dr. Anderson's holistic vision of our profession. This is not just about achieving financial freedom, though that is a significant component; this book is about redefining what it means to be a prosperous and sustainable veterinarian in every sense of the word.

I have had the privilege of knowing Dr. Anderson and the contributing authors for years. I can vouch for their integrity, passion, and success. Each brings a unique perspective that enriches the narrative and offers practical insights that are invaluable. Their stories are not just examples of success but are blueprints for how we can all take control of our lives and careers.

This book challenges us to rethink the status quo, to debunk the myths that have held us back, and to embrace a future where veterinary practices are led by servant leaders who prioritize the well-being of their teams, patients, and communities. The road ahead is not without its challenges, but, as Dr. Anderson so eloquently puts it, taking control of our lives and transforming our profession is well worth the effort.

Transforming our profession means more practices, not fewer, must be either partially or fully owned by veterinarians practicing servant leadership, as Dr. Anderson writes. He and his contributors discuss the ways this can happen in the context of the landscape of today's veterinary profession, and they have much to say—having spent a substantial portion of their time, energy, and experience helping veterinarians achieve ownership.

As someone who has had the privilege of observing Dr. Anderson's journey from the sidelines, I can say with confidence that this book is more than just a guide—it's a manifesto for needed change within our profession. The authors' passion for empowering veterinarians is evident in every word, and their insights have the potential to revolutionize how we approach both our careers and our lives.

Over the years, I've watched as Dr. Anderson has worked tirelessly to bridge the gap between the noble art of veterinary medicine and the often-daunting world of business and finance. It's a mission born out of necessity, as the financial and emotional burdens facing our profession have reached a critical point. His commitment to helping veterinarians not just survive, but thrive, is truly inspiring.

The Prosperous Veterinarian is a testament to that commitment. It's filled with practical advice, real-world examples, and a wealth of knowledge that comes from years of experience.

But more than that, it's a call to action. Dr. Anderson challenges us to take control of our own destinies, to redefine what it means to be successful, and to create a future where prosperity is not just a possibility, but a reality for all veterinarians.

The principles outlined in this book are not just theoretical—they've been tested and proven by Dr. Anderson and his colleagues, whose stories are interwoven throughout the text. These are people who have faced the same challenges we all do, and who have come out on the other side with a deeper understanding of what it means to be prosperous. Their experiences serve as both a guide and a source of inspiration for the rest of us.

As you embark on this journey through the pages of *The Prosperous Veterinarian*, I encourage you to keep an open mind, to practice self-analysis, and to embrace the strategies and philosophies that have been so thoughtfully laid out for you. This is more than just a book; it is a roadmap to a brighter, happier, and more prosperous and sustainable future for all of us in veterinary medicine.

> **This is more than just a book; it is a roadmap to a brighter, happier, and more prosperous and sustainable future for all of us in veterinary medicine.**

In closing, I want to echo the Dr. Anderson's message: the future of our profession is in our hands. By taking control of our lives and embracing the strategies outlined in this book, we can create a brighter, more prosperous future for ourselves and for the generations of veterinarians to follow. The path to that future starts here, with this book, and with the choices we make today.

PREFACE

> "Give a man a fish and you feed him for a day; teach a man to fish and you feed him for a lifetime."
> **LAO TZU**

The fact that you have picked up this book is a great sign for the future of veterinary medicine. For over two decades, I've been translating the language of business and money to veterinarians. Sharing proven principles for taking control of your life and turning ideas into action has become my mission.

During that time, I've gained an appreciation for how our system of education fails to establish basic financial literacy and life-planning skills. There's no encouragement or empowerment to succeed holistically, across clinical, personal, and financial dimensions, and become prosperous.

Ours is an amazing profession with massive potential. We have a built-in Purpose to serve animals and people. Having a Purpose (with a capital P, to emphasize its role as the foundation of our dreams) is key to a well-lived life. We should be thriving! Instead, we are being defined by our student debt burdens, mental health challenges, and unhappiness with the culture of corporate veterinary medicine.

A degree in veterinary medicine is a powerful economic asset that is often underutilized. I've been deeply involved in creating veterinary assets valued at over $1.5 billion and have met or helped many veterinarians progress toward prosperity. I've helped them invest their capital and have discussed many aspects of their lives, including philanthropy, generational wealth, and dreams. Let me assure you, these are wonderful men and women who are doing great work in their communities and are giving back in many ways. They are just like you and me—not one of them started out to make money.

I've learned a great deal from these veterinarians, and I'm indebted to them for sharing their keen insight, stories, and other gifts in this book. I hope you enjoy learning from their experiences as much as I did.

The Prosperous Veterinarian is about far more than money. It is also about personal responsibility, non-financial prosperity, and the tools to live well with success and fulfillment, however you define it. Join us on a path to a brighter, happier future—where you take control of your outcome and transform the experience veterinarians are having throughout our profession.

To that end, I've asked three veterinary colleagues to join me as contributing authors. Jennifer Welser, DVM, DACVO, Chip Cannon, DVM, and Brent Mayabb, DVM are all talented veterinarians who have achieved much success in our profession. They have utilized many of the principles in this book and are uniquely qualified to assist in telling part of our story.

JW I particularly value Jennifer's *("JW")* careful eye and perspective as a woman in veterinary medicine. Jennifer has started practices and lived in the day-to-day of building a veterinary team. She's risen to the very top of corporate veterinary leadership. She has seen all sides of the various business models through which we deliver veterinary care to our patients.

CC Chip *("CC")*, especially, brings a vibrant energy and heart for the soul of our profession. He is an energetic entrepreneur with a passion for real estate investing and has a beautiful family of four girls with his wife, Leah. Chip's passion has been creating ownership opportunities for veterinarians that don't have the capital or business acumen to do it alone. His creativity led to founding CityVet over twenty years ago.

BM Brent's *("BM")* is a unique story of commitment to a strong personal finance discipline that yielded great results. After trying practice early on, Brent chose to work on the "industry" side in animal nutrition. Brent recently acquired a master's degree in personal finance to position himself to help more veterinarians with their financial journey.

The four of us believe you can take control of your life and transform our profession through the application of timeless financial and philosophical principles combined with hard work and the implementation of a Life Operating System ("LOS"). Please note: we make no link between the concepts of "prosperity" and "retirement" as our society defines this term. (Toiling to get to a time of doing nothing for a "25-year self-indulgent vacation" is a fool's errand!)

Throughout the book, we confront the hard topic (for vets) of the money component of prosperity right up front. Through our conversations with veterinarians, we know that they define prosperity as *freedom*. We agree! When we discuss wealth and financial prosperity throughout the book, we do so in the context of achieving financial freedom. We also spend time exploring the concept of **comprehensive prosperity** to include its financial and non-financial components. We hope you forgive our blending of these concepts throughout the book, as we see them as a unified objective.

Ultimately, we believe that to transform our profession, more practices – not fewer – must be either partially or fully-owned by veterinarians practicing *servant leadership*. We discuss the ways this can happen in the context of today's veterinary economic landscape, and we have a lot say— having spent a significant portion of our time and energy helping veterinarians achieve ownership.

Along the way, we debunk some programming you may have received earlier in your life, so keep an open mind and practice self-analysis. There are no sacred cows on our journey. In sharing various examples of colleagues who pursued prosperity, we highlight the approaches they used to take control of their future and the environments they created for their practices and veterinary teams.

We also give you a practical approach to building your own prosperity and tactics around planning and executing what we've outlined as a "Life Plan." Lastly, we even journey into a useful, pragmatic philosophy and material to anchor you in the inevitable storms that visit our lives.

Taking control of our lives and transforming our profession is worth the effort, for our families, patients, teams, communities, and future generations of veterinarians. We are at an inflection point in our journey. How we behave in the next decade-plus can restore the veterinary profession and its culture to its former brilliance. You have great power to contribute to this narrative, and along the way become a happier, more fulfilled, and prosperous veterinarian.

Onward!

Yours in prosperity,
Andy Anderson
August 2024

CHAPTER 1

THE VETERINARY DEGREE AS AN ENGINE OF PROSPERITY

By Andy Anderson

"I just want to say thank you."
　　On the phone was Dr. Katy, a veterinarian based in a mid-size US city. In her early 30s, she had spent the first part of her career working within a larger practice as a clinician until it was acquired by a corporate entity. Like many of the dozens of veterinarians we've partnered with, she loved animals, was focused on developing her skills, and was committed to providing the best care possible. But she faced a dilemma—would she stay in the corporate gig, go work for someone else at another clinic, or branch out on her own?

　　Katy most of all wanted to run her own practice. In some ways, though, she felt stuck. She worried about the many aspects of running a practice that were unfamiliar to her. Where would she get the know-how she needed?

Despite great online reviews and a loyal customer base, running a business can present innumerable obstacles. For some vets, it seems like every month they're on the verge of "burning out"—even when they are only serving as a clinician. How could someone possibly handle the whole operation, plus meet student debt payments? It can be overwhelming.

It's common for new practice owners to basically live "paycheck to paycheck." When you're not at the clinic, you're not making any money. And what about long-term? How do you grow the practice and actually build wealth so you don't have to work full-time until you drop dead?

> **How do you grow the practice and actually build wealth so you don't have to work full-time until you drop dead?**

Katy's situation isn't unique. Many veterinarians struggle to do it all. And by "do it all," I mean providing great care while managing stress and developing the economic side of their practice.

On the surface, a veterinarian's struggles seem to align with the "conventional wisdom" about our profession. I'm sure you've heard it all before:

- *Veterinarians don't make much money.*
- *Veterinarians aren't good at business.*
- *Veterinarians are too charitable to ever be successful.*

So goes the "conventional wisdom." We may even believe it about ourselves. But is any of it *really true*?

There *are* a few truths about our profession. We love animals and providing care—that's a fact. But sadly, we share another common denominator: *debt*. Today, veterinary school graduates are graduating with six-figure debt and facing decades before they can pay it off.

Perhaps it's this debt burden that drains our confidence in our business acumen. Perhaps it's other changes in the field. A generation ago, statistically, the typical veterinarian was a man, a small business owner, a visible member of the community, and generally happy. Today, of the approximately 125,000 veterinarians in the US, nearly 70 percent are women.[1] Veterinarians nowadays are more likely to work part-time, be an employee of a corporate entity, and – heartbreakingly – experience mental health challenges like depression.

What was once a profession of personal and financial fulfillment is drifting toward becoming, in many ways, just another "job." Like the pharmacist at the national chain drugstore down the street, we are in danger of becoming akin to hourly workers, cogs in a corporate machine. Has our profession become a less attractive career for the brightest young people to pursue?

Amassing massive student debt, confronting the realities of the practice, the shock of euthanizing pets nonstop—it's no

---

1 "U.S. Veterinarian Numbers." 2023. American Veterinary Medical Association (AVMA). December 31, 2023. https://www.avma.org/resources-tools/reports-statistics/market-research-statistics-us-veterinarians.

wonder that the industry has a high suicide rate.[2] These negative trends are distressing and alarming—and must be changed.

But, again, do these trends exist because veterinarians are *bad* at business? Are we destined to give *everything* and get little financial reward in return?

Heck no. We can take control of our lives, be happier, and in the process secure our profession's future!

As a veterinarian, a founder of multiple practices, a former treasurer of the American College of Veterinary Surgeons, and the executive chairman of CityVet and Arista Advanced Pet Care, I've developed a unique understanding of veterinary medicine and veterinarians. I've also built multiple $100-plus million veterinary enterprises, worked for large financial institutions, and graduated from Harvard Business School.

I can tell you, without a doubt, that we veterinarians are a supremely capable bunch. While building prosperity or enjoying success in business and investing may not be the reasons we get out of bed in the morning, I've learned firsthand how our profession is uniquely suited to these pursuits and many others.

Let's get back to the story of Dr. Katy. Despite her feeling of being stuck, it turned out she was in a prime position to become a prosperous veterinarian. She had the essential ingredients at hand: the clinical skills, the work ethic, the location, and the willingness to co-create as a partner. With the help of CityVet, a general practice growth engine building practices

---

2 Spidel, Anna. 2023. "Why Suicide Rates Are High Among Veterinary Professionals." NPR, December 19, 2023. https://www.npr.org/2023/12/19/1220443869/why-suicide-rates-are-high-among-veterinary-professionals.

in partnership with individual veterinarians, she was able to co-create a clinic that did general practice and urgent care, allowing her to build wealth, develop her leadership skills, and obtain financial freedom.

Two years after partnering with her, she gave me that phone call to say thanks. "I personally made $40,000 last month," she said, excitement in her voice. Of course, after the lean years, the money was certainly welcome—but in her voice I also heard relief, pride, and confidence in her family's future.

Dr. Katy's "do it all" concerns were over. She hadn't needed to compromise and work in a corporate practice or for someone else's practice. She had gone from stuck to in control of her practice and career—and now she was maximizing its potential for prosperity while serving others.

> **In her voice I also heard relief, pride, and confidence in her family's future. Dr. Katy's "do it all" concerns were over.**

It's safe to say her practice has become wildly successful. Since adding urgent care hours, the business is 50 percent larger, and has an annual growth rate over 30 percent. All that has translated into real income. (From an initial small equity investment plus loans provided by CityVet, her practice is now likely worth $6-8 million.)

Last but not least, Katy had a beautiful baby boy right when she started the new practice. She raised the newborn while getting the practice humming. Thankfully, everything went so well that she's paid off her student loans, her home mortgage—and, today, is opening a second location.

We have many success stories like Dr. Katy's, but this book isn't about CityVet or Arista. Instead, I undertook this project to open your mind to new possibilities and give you the tools to pursue them. For veterinarians, by veterinarians—we wrote *The Prosperous Veterinarian* to share the common struggles and present solutions available for *everyone* willing to seize the opportunities at hand

Ultimately, my hope is to rewrite the conventional wisdom about the profession we love. To all current and future veterinarians, please know this:

- *We can be as successful and happy as we want to be.*
- *We can be great at leading our practices and mentoring future vets.*
- *We can achieve comprehensive prosperity.*

These outcomes are just a few turned pages (and some focused work) away. In the meantime, please know there's hope for veterinarians everywhere to enjoy the fruits of their investment in education and commitment to service. There are many aspects to this that we'll cover in the chapters ahead. But the journey starts with seeing the veterinary degree for what it really is: an engine of tremendous economic prosperity and service potential.

Let's rewind the clock to graduation day. When they called your name and you walked across the stage to receive your veterinary degree, you were hoping the diploma granted you the respect, responsibility, and opportunity for a career you were passionate about.

But did you know that in addition to those rewards, you also received your right to a share of the $150-plus billion pet care industry? (Not to mention your access to the $23 trillion US economy.) In other words, there's opportunity all around you, and you are among a uniquely positioned, insulated class of professionals with significant barriers to others competing against you. The power of this protected position cannot be understated!

As a practicing veterinarian, you are held to the standards of practice and continuing education to maintain this protected status. Other than that, you are free to pursue your dreams in this well-insulated sandbox. The only limits are those you set for yourself.

I say all this because, too often, graduates are so overwhelmed with debt that they can't see their proximity to prosperity. They don't see their degree for the economic engine that it is.

When I say engine, I mean a purposefully-designed, self-perpetuating mechanism to build and maintain your prosperity. It's your choice to:

- Keep the engine small but well-maintained
- Boost its horsepower

- Rebuild it as a jet engine
- Connect it to other jet engines to go stratospheric

The bottom line is this: when it comes to developing your engine, the opportunities are *limitless*.

Building Prosperity

You are a veterinarian, not a professional in the finance industry. But there are a few universal principles that we must understand and apply if we want to achieve financial freedom and comprehensive prosperity as a veterinarian.

Foremost, it's essential to become a productive and highly capable clinician. We must first excel at our profession if we're to use it to build prosperity. (Remember—*this* is your economic engine). You're likely on your way to checking that box already.

Second, I encourage every veterinarian (if you haven't done so) to take a basic personal finance course. They are available online or at your local community college. These courses form the foundation of wealth-building. They include the basics of budgeting, insurance (use sparingly), mortgages and other consumer debt, investing, and estate-planning. Please keep in mind that these courses are for the masses and very few people taking them have the economic engine you possess. That said you can't move forward without establishing the basics of Personal Finance 101.

Third, we must learn the concepts of money and value creation, as well as the path to a happier life, that we describe in this book. There are a few recurring themes of life and prosperity in the stories of Dr. Katy and other veterinarians we share—hopefully you'll see how these apply to your situation. My goal is for you to have these realizations:

- You can build a practice that you have ownership in.
- You can invest intelligently in the public equity market.
- You can own and benefit from commercial properties.
- You can generate passive cash-flow from savings, investments, practices, and ventures beyond veterinary medicine.
- You can truly enjoy the non-financial aspects of prosperity, such as living a Purpose-based life, building a family, having long-term friendships, being anchored in faith and spirituality, and giving back.
- You can be happier *and* prosperous.

Fourth, we must *apply* what we learn. We must take action to pursue and benefit from passive income, such as dividends, interest, rental property proceeds, and business earnings not directly tied to our labor. In order to do this effectively, you must develop a *Life Plan* that incorporates what matters most to you and charts an intentional path to your comprehensive prosperity.

Here's the simple goal: being debt free and having your passive income surpass your expenses. At such a point, your *passive cash flow* allows you to pursue your dreams, fulfill your Purpose, and help others—*without* trading your time for money. Dr. Katy did it in her thirties. You can too!

SOLVING THE "DEBT PROBLEM"

Our profession is applying significant time, energy, and resources into solving the veterinary debt problem. Newly minted veterinarians can have up to $500,000 in debt, with the AVMA reporting an average of $150,000-$200,000.[3]

To combat such a debt burden, some employers are trying to attract and keep staff by offering debt relief programs—typically up to a couple hundred dollars a month to go toward debt. In addition, the AVMA is known to support public service loan forgiveness and debt repayment programs.[4] Some veterinarians are making their debt payments through 20 to 25-year repayment terms and then hoping the remainder, at some point, will be forgiven without tax implications.

In my experience, debt is a symptom, not the main problem. The problem can only be addressed by building our own wealth and implementing tried-and-true budgeting, discipline, and financial techniques.

If you have significant debt (six figures) and you don't have a detailed budget geared towards retiring that debt completely within 10 years, then you must get started. The steps you need to take will cause some pain. But putting an extra $100 a month to paying off your principal is better

---

[3] "Veterinary Starting Salaries Rise in 2023, Educational Debt Holds Steady." 2023. American Veterinary Medical Association. November 1, 2023. https://www.avma.org/news/veterinary-starting-salaries-rise-2023-educational-debt-holds-steady.

[4] "Student Loan Forgiveness and Repayment Programs." n.d. American Veterinary Medical Association. https://www.avma.org/resources-tools/personal-finance/student-loan-forgiveness-repayment-programs.

than anything else you can spend it on. Brent's story, in Chapter 4, shows how he and his wife repaid all of their student debt and saved a significant nest egg in under fifteen years. They both worked but chose to live off one salary, allowing the other's income to be used for building an emergency fund and accelerating debt repayment.

The prosperity producing principles presented in the chapters ahead will make minced meat of your student debt and leave you wondering why you spent all those hours stressing about it.

Why would we want to cede our financial outcome to the government or corporate employers? Why would we not take responsibility for our debts and unleash our engine of prosperity to repay the debt *and* create substantial prosperity for ourselves and our families?

Wealth-*Multiplying* vs. Wealth-*Building* Careers

Let's examine a few of the possibilities for unleashing your engine of prosperity on the world. These possibilities can be boiled down to two types: wealth-multiplying and wealth-building activities or careers. You will have to decide for yourself which is best for you.

Wealth-building careers are the standard roles of "non-owners" and are certain to produce an adequate and even very comfortable level of income. In the case of veterinarians working in these activities, if they are frugal, strong savers, and invest well, they could build wealth and enjoy a comfortable, cost-conscious retirement. (I've even seen plenty of cases of multi-million-dollar portfolios from simply saving and investing well.)

Wealth-Building Careers

- Associate Veterinarian
- Lead Veterinarian
- Medical Director
- CEO of someone else's business (unless it's really big, think Zoetis)
- Chief Medical Officer for someone else's practice
- Professor
- Consultant
- Researcher
- Sales and marketing

The common denominator of these great careers is that, in the end, they have you spending your career "trading your hours for someone else's dollars."

Then there are the wealth-*multiplying* activities and careers. These are the difference-makers, producing "cash flow streams" that end in transformational prosperity.

Wealth-Multiplying Careers

- Practice Owner (1-100% ownership)
- Multi-practice Owner (1-100% ownership)
- Practice Real Estate owner

- Small Business Owner (non-vet practice)
- Commercial Real Estate owner/developer
- Inventor
- Software Developer for sale to others
- Venture Capital/Private Investor with ownership

Here is the principle we must learn: **Cash-Flow Streams (CFS) are the ultimate source of economic value.** In particular, we must pursue CFS that don't require us to be present in the operating room or exam room. The most amazing thing about these passive income activities and the assets they produce is that they are not worth just the cash flow they produce in one year but *many multiples of the one-year cash flow.*

Consider Dr. Katy's veterinary practice that makes $1,000,000 in cash flow after all expenses including the owner's compensation for work performed as a clinician and manager. In today's market, her practice is likely worth $6-8 million or more. Amazing!

The same multiplier effect is true for commercial real estate assets, other small businesses, royalties, and stocks. Many factors affect the multiple of cash flow that assets are worth, but two of the most important are *growth potential* and *predictability*. Fortunately, these two factors are within the control of the owner and management of these businesses.

A Win-Win Path

I was in my twenties when I first realized that wealth was something I could build. Back then I knew next to nothing about money (other than how to spend it). What I did have a sense for was this truth: *life would be much easier and more fun if I had the resources to navigate it on my own terms.* In other words, financial prosperity was central to providing not only stability but also flexibility and, in its truest form, freedom.

I started college intent on becoming a vet. Then, in pursuit of financial wealth, I gave up on veterinary school and went into business, perceiving that the financial opportunities in veterinary medicine were inadequate. I was in my late twenties when I finally realized another truth: *financial wealth wasn't everything and that my goal was* **comprehensive prosperity**.

Neglecting my passion for veterinary medicine to compete in the traditional winner-take-all world of business didn't sit right with me. I didn't like the "zero sum" nature of that world. I believed I could find a way to apply my God-given talents so that both parties in an encounter could win ("win-win"). My wife, Kim, was such a wonderful contributor to rethinking my career at this time of life. (As I write this, in 2024, we've just celebrated 36 years of marriage.) She's a great listener, thinker, and thought partner in terms of analyzing what is true prosperity and what makes a happy life. I remember her wisdom in saying, "you know I'd rather have you happy with modest resources than miserable with a lot of money." As Warren Buffett says, "choosing a partner in life is the most important decision you'll ever make," and I agree.

Building a complete and happy life, a prosperous life (that includes resources to follow your chosen path and make your mark), always includes the non-financial components: family, friends, faith, community, health, and giving back alongside your work. The question Kim and I solved for during our journey became: *How do we pursue our Purpose and build comprehensive prosperity that's a win-win at the same time?* Our answer was to return to my passion of veterinary medicine and have faith that God would lead us to a prosperous place.

At 32, I reapplied to veterinary school. I was one of the oldest in my class, but with my age also came with experience. I had a Harvard MBA, Wall Street experience, and a lot of exposure to businesses and organizations. The best part, for me, was that after I graduated—and completed another four years of training to become a board-certified small animal surgeon—I knew exactly what I wanted and was ready to get started at age 40!

Focused on being a great veterinarian, I also knew that I could simultaneously pursue a wealth-building career. In pursuit of the win-win, I founded a practice with Fred Williams, my first partner—later in the book we'll cover the value of business partnerships, which (like the engine of prosperity) are an asset that can provide substantial returns. One of the most important aspects of my career has been my many great partners, and that started with Fred, who brought a plethora of complementary skills to our new endeavor. Soon after we started our first practice in San Antonio, it became very successful—so we opened a couple more in Houston, again with great veterinary partners, Dr. Justin Payne and Dr. John Dahlinger, who did the heavy lifting in their markets.

In opening our practices, we applied the lessons and principles from this book, and our success truly snowballed. Within a few short years—I was in my late forties—I finally achieved financial freedom. At last, I was a prosperous veterinarian. (For me, some of the non-financial components of comprehensive prosperity have required consistent long-term effort. I'm happy to report I'm making solid progress and seeking continuous improvement on those pieces as well.)

Today, I write this from a bison ranch in the Texas hill country. Freedom for me has allowed me to pursue my passion of raising bison while working on things that serve my Purpose of *Learning, Sharing, and Serving*. To that end, I'm grateful to have spent the past few years serving a non-profit biomedical research institute, my church, and others with their journeys in business and personal development.

Our goal in writing *The Prosperous Veterinarian* is to help as many of the 125,000-plus veterinarians as possible enjoy freedom and happiness through the application of the principles and tools found within these pages. While many veterinarians may not find the path laid out in this book realistic or even desirable, we offer our support for your journey, and we hope you can find something useful in this work.

There's more to my story, and more to learn from the stories of the many other veterinarians we feature in the chapters ahead. But as we close out this chapter, I hope you've learned the one ultimate truth: *you* possess everything you need to obtain financial freedom, be happier, and become a prosperous veterinarian.

It's time to lean on your engine's throttle.

CHAPTER 2

THE VETERINARIAN'S DYSFUNCTIONAL RELATIONSHIP WITH MONEY

by Jennifer Welser and Andy Anderson

"Don't you see how much you have to offer?
And yet you still settle for less."
MARCUS AURELIUS

 For years I had a dysfunctional relationship with money (and I'm still working on it). Personally and professionally, it wasn't a primary focus. I'm a veterinarian, after all, not in it for the riches.

I was brought up in a financially stable household where you didn't talk about money other than to say it had to be earned and you should live within your means. I was fortunate to graduate from veterinary school in the mid-1990s before the cost of education skyrocketed. I had no debt from undergrad and very manageable debt from veterinary school. I entered the professional work world ready to make a living—and completely avoid thinking about money.

But no matter how much we try to avoid it, money is an inescapable, ever-present part of our life.

> **No matter how much we try to avoid it, money is an inescapable, ever-present part of our life.**

In the veterinary world, there are constant reminders. One that always gets me can be heard every day. No pet owner ever tells a story about visiting their veterinarian without eventually talking about the *cost*. They can tell the whole story, and you're just waiting for it—the moment when they mention the price. The outcome for their pet can be good or bad, they can love or be mad at their vet, and the amount may or may not create a financial hardship for them. And still the cost of care always comes up. This constant association between pet care and cost is ingrained in people's minds. Even if someone has ample funds, they never say, "Oh, it seemed *too* cheap considering everything they did for my pet."

Even my attorney, charging me a hefty hourly rate, once told me about how her cat was diagnosed with early renal failure and he had to spend the night in the hospital on fluids. Then she casually mentioned, "I couldn't believe it was $705." I couldn't help but point out to her that the cost was less than *two* hours of her time, yet her cat was seen by a veterinarian and received 24 hours of care at the hospital.

There's such a disconnect attached to the cost of care. Everyone understands that human healthcare is expensive, but the insurance and billing system make it impossible to connect specific costs with specific diagnostics or treatments at the time of care. Whereas in the veterinary office, a client is given a bill and has to open their pocketbook each time, making it impossible *not* to connect the costs with the care. And that's just the tip of the iceberg when it comes to the dysfunctional relationship many veterinarians have with money.

It's no secret—the business aspects of being a veterinarian are often treated as an afterthought. Even though many veterinary students may end up becoming business owners, schools don't fully prioritize time and space in a curriculum to emphasize learning essential business skills.

For me, I paid little attention to the money side until I had to. Even then, it took a while before I gave it my full attention. After I left a salaried position and began independently contracting ophthalmology services to multi-specialty hospitals, I started hiring and managing my own staff, handling their payroll, buying and managing my own equipment and supplies, and navigating service contracts. I didn't have to directly handle client billing or care for the facility, but I did pay a hefty percent to the hospital to manage that end. Then I just kept whatever was leftover. But with all those expenses adding up, I had no choice but to start thinking about money differently.

What I gradually began to discover was that the more I learned about the business, money, and financial health of my practice, the less I stressed *and* the healthier the practice was. Eventually, managing (most) of the business side became something I enjoyed, and my relationship with money started becoming functional. Of course, guilt also set in when I started making what felt like was quite a bit of money. This was, after all, money coming from the pockets of pet owners. (Guilt is a topic unto itself!)

The next breakthroughs in my dysfunctional money relationships came after I joined what would become BluePearl Veterinary Partners, the national specialty referral and emergency hospital company. I invested a little bit of money in the business by trading all of my ophthalmology equipment to BluePearl for half cash and half shares. Looking back, I should have taken it all in shares, but I was naïve and entirely uneducated in terms of investing and what equity could mean to my finances.

The hospital administrator at BluePearl at the time, Dave G., enjoyed teaching the doctors about business basics and personal finance. From him we learned about calculating a return on investment (ROI) and had fun doing it. Dave also got to see firsthand just how avoidant and dysfunctional veterinarians can be about money. He once tried to start a finance club and asked us all to come to the first meeting with a stock tip. That was a bit advanced for us—instead, we all showed up needing the basics on how to manage debt, start saving for retirement, and understand the meaning of being a shareholder in BluePearl. Many of us became much savvier about business and money thanks to him. Dave also tried hard to teach us not to take client complaints and refund requests as a personal attack but rather as part of being in healthcare services.

Feeling responsibility and accountability for our patients and clients is engrained in us. And part of our money dysfunction is not being able to feel good about caring and doing our best even when an outcome isn't perfect. Building resilience and coping skills when feeling attacked by a client, regardless of the circumstances, is part of our journey.

Veterinarians are inherently learners, always seeking to expand our knowledge. But when it comes to finances, many of us feel intimidated. It's unfamiliar territory. There's a new vocabulary to learn, with new ideas, which makes it seem like there are layers of complexity to understanding money.

There is also a notion that we need to master financial concepts perfectly before we can even begin to engage with them, which can feel unrealistic and overwhelming. Unlike making medical decisions where we're comfortable with both the known and the unknown, we treat financial matters as something that demands absolute comprehension. That is unrealistic.

Instead, we need to shift our mindset towards learning financial skills as we would any other aspect of our profession—recognizing that it's okay not to know everything, the importance of continuously learning, and working with others who have skills that we don't. In other words, we must prioritize the financial side of our business and personal lives as much as we prioritize the quality of care we provide.

The bottom-line: The healthier our relationship with money, the healthier it is for us and those we serve.

EVERY DECISION INVOLVES A MONEY DECISION

AA Veterinarians are driven by *Purpose*. We want to heal animals and serve people. We have somehow understood the act of pursuing prosperity to *conflict* with our Purpose. We can't be purpose-driven *and* wealth-driven, can we? But nothing could be further from the truth.

Our goal is to help you realize that becoming prosperous and meeting the highest ideals of our profession are not in conflict.

As a veterinarian (or other healthcare professional) you have been endowed with tremendous responsibility and opportunity. The responsibility is to deliver the best care to your clients at a fair price consistent within the market context where you practice. The opportunity is to maximize the fair return on your investment in education, professional development, equipment, facilities, staff, and other assets.

Your time is valuable. I can assure you that your clients and everyone with whom you transact thinks *their* time and service is valuable, too. They don't discount their services just because Dr. So-And-So is nice. Their expectation is that they are seeking our services for a fair fee.

As veterinarians, consideration of the financial implications is often non-existent in our decision making (or at best an afterthought). Consider your analysis of the cost of becoming a veterinarian. We'll wager that you conducted very little financial analysis of the debt obligation you would incur versus your future income and expenses. Perhaps the answer would have given you pause before the whiff of formalin hit you walking into the anatomy lab for the first time.

We all live on the continuum between the "practical" and the "ideal." In choosing veterinary medicine, we were very much standing on the "ideal" end of the continuum. Money was decidedly secondary.

That being said, our goal for you is to apply a financial lens to all major (and most minor) decisions in life. This is not to advocate for an "everything comes down to money" approach, but rather to encourage that money should account for at least an equally weighted place in one's analytic framework of life.

I'm reminded of Jordan B. Peterson's 2nd rule in his wonderful book, *The 12 Rules of Life: An Antidote for Chaos*: "Treat yourself like someone you are responsible for helping." Consider yourself as a patient. Would you move forward with a major treatment plan without a review of some lab work or imaging? Certainly, the entirety of the decision would not be based solely on one diagnostic category but rather on a thoughtful assessment of the total picture. The financial impact is but one (albeit a significant one) of the things you must consider.

Here is an example. Within the different veterinary specialty disciplines there exists substantial differences in what people earn. Surgeons and ophthalmologists are highest and medical disciplines tend to be lower. I remember a conversation with "Janet," a colleague who was frustrated by income differences as compared to higher paid colleagues. I asked her if she had accounted for that when she chose to do a residency in her discipline. She replied, "I never even considered it."

At that moment, Janet realized she had to start at least considering the financial implications of her future decisions. Her choice had resulted in millions of dollars of less earnings over her lifetime. Even with thoughtful analysis, she may have made the same choice, but at least she would have gone in "eyes wide open." This conversation led her on the path to become much more financially astute and very successful. Today she has financial freedom and is doing great pursuing her passion of mentoring younger veterinarians.

Our Money Dysfunctions

JW We know money is an inescapable part of life. So to have a healthier relationship with it, we must identify and talk about some of the common dysfunctions many of us share:

- *Guilt*
- *Misguided beliefs and biases we have about money*

- *The narrative that we're "not good at" business or money*
- *Fear, avoidance, and negatively repeating personal soundtracks preventing us from finding resilience and joy in our work*
- *"Defeatism" in the face of debt or loss of control*
- *Being our own worst enemy*
- *The idea that making good money as a veterinarian is unethical*

First off, we veterinarians have a "guilt" issue when it comes to money or charging fairly for our services and talents. We wonder where this "guilt" originates. Let's look at three facts.

1. *Money is both a medium of exchange for goods and services and a store of value.* Money and wealth are a product of work, intelligence, character, and creativity. These are all traits that we as veterinarians have in great supply that are often underutilized.
2. *Veterinarians are vital participants in the economic system of the country.* We buy products from drug companies and equipment manufacturers. We rent commercial real estate, pay lawn services, utility bills, taxes, and so much more. Why would we believe we are somehow not worthy of fair compensation for our work, intellectual property, and talents? All the counter-parties in our business transactions are seeking to create the most profit and highest fair economic return for themselves and their employers—and so should we. Having dis-

posable income means we also put money back into the system when we buy and renovate homes, travel, or seek entertainment.

3. *Pet ownership is a choice, similar to having children.* Pet ownership comes with responsibilities, including many that are expensive. Veterinary care is part of those expenses and we as a profession must provide a range of care solutions from which consumers may choose. There are many ways we can give back and make sure there are options accessible to low-income pet owners. It is not our fault that care carries economic costs or that we must earn a return on our investments to continue to sustain our families and businesses.

Bury the guilt! Holding on to it would be like an anchor and your chances of being financially independent and free would die on the vine. It would be like pouring syrup in your engine of prosperity, slowing you down to a sputter. Be fair, be ethical, *and* bury the guilt.

WHAT'S YOUR ATTITUDE?

For any relationship to be functional, we must know our predisposed attitude toward the relationship. We must be aware of our biases and beliefs that we bring to the table.

Psychologists Brad and Ted Klontz have published research based on their construct of the four most prevalent attitudes about money. They call these narratives in our head, "money scripts."[5,6] Brad's and Ted's work demonstrates the four most important *money scripts* are:

- *Money Avoidance*
- *Money Worship*
- *Money Status*
- *Money Vigilance*

In our experience, *Money Avoidance* is the most prevalent money script for veterinarians. *Money Avoidance* carries beliefs and biases such as:

- Rich people are greedy.
- People get rich by taking advantage of others.
- Money corrupts people.
- Good people shouldn't care about money.

Of course, there are many examples of rich people doing bad things to help reinforce a Money Avoidance bias. But at the same time, the data supports that these ideas lead to lower income, lower net worth, less education, and other money disorders.

A money avoidant perspective also makes it easier to accept your lack of wealth as somehow virtuous. Nothing could be further from the truth. Rich people are people

---

5 You can listen to Brad on YouTube and even take a free assessment at www.bradklontz.com.

6 Find your own money script here: https://www.yourmentalwealthadvisors.com/our-process/your-money-script/

just like you—only with more money. Some are bad while most are good, like any other subset of human beings.

I assume you are a good person and that you have good intentions in acquiring and applying the principles of this book. The good news is that you can remain a good person while applying the prosperity-generating principles of this book.

There are plenty of examples of people who obtained financial freedom by acquiring knowledge and skills, working really hard, then saving and investing capital. The most successful then can apply their wealth to solving problems, taking care of others, and leaving it to charities and future generations.

For most of us, our money perspective was developed during our formative years. The Klontzs' work identifies that we all have financial flashpoint events that help define our money scripts.

From a personal perspective, one of my flashpoints was watching my father's experience with risk-avoidance behavior. My father was a wonderful, hardworking man and a child of the Great Depression. He came from a broken home in small-town Texas, where a single mother raised him while working three jobs. Clearly, he had seen a lot of hardship and scarcity, wherein he forged a clear bias to avoid losing any money. He was smart and pushed through this stifling narrative enough to engage in some investing activities.

Following his WWII service, Dad had only two subsequent jobs. The first lasted two years and the second thirty-eight years. He rose from the warehouse to sales to the leadership of a $100 million business as its CEO. Sounds impressive, and it produced a comfortable lifestyle for our family growing up. But know this—his wealth outcome was only a fraction of what it could have been, and this turned out to have a great impact on my view of risk and investing. "Here," as the immortal Paul Harvey might say, "is the rest of the story."

About ten years into my father's tenure at his company, the owner was dying. He approached my father and, in appreciation of his service, said he wanted to sell him the business. The price was $1.0 million. An astronomical sum and what seemed unapproachable to a 40-year-old from a poor background and risk averse mindset. Nevertheless, my father went to work speaking with bankers and friends. He found the money, but he would have to sign a $1.0 million loan. This was more than his net worth and he viewed it as risking everything. It really wasn't an all-or-nothing risk, but the psychological hurdle was just too great.

Ultimately, Dad had to pass up the opportunity and the business was sold to an insurance company that had a portfolio of operating companies. My father became the CEO for the next 28 years and when he retired the company was worth over $50 million. His story became a part of my education on the importance of asset ownership. My father's experience became my blessing. I think he died thinking I took too much risk but celebrating my success and knowing he had a part in it.

How do you feel about money? It's a very personal decision. It will likely evolve as your needs grow and your financial maturity accelerates through experience. Many factors affect your financial literacy including your family values, education, and self-esteem. As Brad Klontz, says, "the money scripts people have in their head were often learned in childhood, are unconscious, passed down through generations, just partial truths, and are responsible for our financial outcomes."

It can be truly rewarding to see what sort of money scripts you are holding on to, and to make sure these don't hold you back from prosperity. Please take the money scripts test and spend some time understanding those events that have shaped your view of money. The Klontz's book, *Mind over Money: Overcoming the Money Disorders That Threaten Our Financial Health*, is excellent. (If you don't invest in reading it, at least listen to Brad on YouTube.)

In his now classic book, *Rich Dad, Poor Dad*, (first written in 1997), author Robert Kiyosaki recounts the experiences and lessons learned from two influential men in his life. His "Poor Dad" and biological father was anything but poor. He was highly educated (Stanford, University of Chicago) and earned a good living as a high-ranking government employee. He was "poor" in the sense of lacking any knowledge on how to convert his skills to financial security. On the other hand, his best friend's father became his "Rich Dad" and shared the insights of wealth creation and how behavior toward money can make an enormous difference in one's outcome.

I share Robert's frustration with our education system's lack of success in teaching practical financial literacy and relegating so many to a life devoid of financial security. As veterinarians, we value education and the acquisition of skills. Through this book we hope to pay into the bankrupt financial education account of our profession.

Robert's dads often had opposing attitudes, for example; the Poor Dad would espouse, "the government needs to have the rich pay more in taxes," while the Rich Dad would say, "taxes punish those who produce the most and reward those who don't produce." By taking money away from the producers we are removing fuel from the most productive people in the economy and giving it to the government, which is perhaps the most inefficient and hapless allocator of capital.

Robert and his friend both ended up following the Rich Dad's advice. The results were rather amazing and each created substantial wealth, freedom, and good works in their respective fields. While a few of Robert's insights today may read dated, the major pillars of his work are intact. I encourage each of you to read Robert's book. It will help reinforce the concepts we present and allow you to hear these fundamental truths in a different voice.

Paying particular attention to the Poor Dad's perspectives might help you to see some similarities with your programming. Overcoming dysfunctional success narratives is an important step in taking control of your life and securing the bright future you and your family deserve.

Get Out of Your Own Way!

JW It's a powerful realization for veterinarians, especially those reaching the mid-point of their careers, to understand that developing a healthy relationship with money is attainable and often just a few adjustments away. Don't get down on yourself: it is never too late. The journey to financial literacy isn't insurmountable—it's more about recognizing and addressing certain dysfunctions or gaps in understanding (such as with the "money scripts").

This transition to becoming financially literate is not just about gaining more knowledge or skills, but also about overcoming the internal barriers that veterinarians often face, such as self-doubt or hesitation to ask for clarification when financial concepts aren't clear. You are *not* at the mercy of external forces. You *can* truly shape your dream career.

Yes, it requires effort, persistence, and maybe even grinding it out at times, but support is available, opportunities abound, and you don't need to surrender your life. Knowledge and freedom of choice presents an empowering path where you control your destiny.

This empowerment is the secret strength of this book. It shows you that you hold the power. And realizing this, you may be able to look at work and life a bit differently. What might have been viewed as sacrifice can be viewed as a fulfilling path to a significantly brighter, happier, and more prosperous future.

Emotional Resilience

Today, our trade publications continue to be filled with articles about mental health, compassion fatigue, and shocking suicide rates. We are at least making progress in destigmatizing discussions about mental health and well-being. Interestingly, a lack of "work-life balance" is frequently cited as the major cause of burnout. With the focus on work-life balance, there is almost the implication of a strict cutoff in working hours rather than a focus on whether a person is healthy and finding joy and fulfillment in their work *and* life.

"Work" isn't a four-letter word. Gardeners go work in their yard. Artists go work in a studio. Athletes work tirelessly at their sport. And raising children isn't play—it's work. Hard work – of all sorts, whether for compensation or not – can be a great source of fulfillment and pride.

Dr. Paul Kline, chief veterinary officer, spends a good portion of his time coaching partners and their teams on how to address everyday stresses in their practices. He often expresses his frustration with the use of the term "work-life balance." He argues that the opposite of work should be rest, not life. He advocates for a *work-rest balance.*

Are you working adequately and joyfully? Do you have control over and the means to work at your life—travel, play, rest, enjoy hobbies? What is your play? This broader picture includes work, play, sleep, eating, family—all essential components of life. Thus, work is not balanced against life;

rather, work is balanced against *rest*, which seems to be a more holistic approach.

At the same time, the more you're making your money work for you (rather than you for it), the less you'll think about "work-life balance." When you're earning more and working less through passive income, then you can have true balance that comes from prosperity.

You're in the Driver's Seat

On the surface, a career in veterinary medicine may seem less attractive today than it was a generation ago. The cost of education, the messaging about high burnout, the "low pay," and the lack of understanding about all of the opportunities the degree can offer are just some of the reasons. But the truth is this—veterinary medicine is and can be an attractive career for anyone with a love of animals, people, health, and the planet. The more who see this truth, the better.

If you feel stuck in a dead-end job or overwhelmed with your current situation, look up, look out, and learn. Let me explain. For veterinarians who operate largely on a fee-for-service basis, when you're not working, you're not making money. Your income is not just tied to your skill and effort, but also to your continuous physical availability. Going on vacation? Don't expect a paycheck.

This situation contributes to burnout, because taking a break is directly tied to financial stability. Taking a vacation isn't just a simple matter of relaxing; it has tangible financial repercussions due to the lack of income generation during that time.

> **If you feel stuck in a dead-end job or overwhelmed with your current situation, look up, look out, and learn.**

These short-term issues worsen in the long term. Lacking a solid long-term financial plan or investments can lead to a precarious financial future. You might enjoy a comfortable lifestyle for now, but without strategic saving or investing, your long-term financial health could be at risk as more demands pile up—such as raising kids, college expenses, elder care, and your own retirement.

In other words, working "hourly" caps your lifetime earnings at a fraction of what you could be earning as an investor, entrepreneur, and/or business owner. The good news: you're in the driver's seat.

Sometimes the difference between a multi-million career and a dead-end job is a simple change in ZIP code. There are current realities in our profession such as non-competes tying you to a job and a geography. Not trying to ignore the importance of community and where you have grown roots, but would you relocate if you had the prospects to become prosperous and have more control?

The difference might also be in taking a class or reading books to learn about personal finance or investing, developing the self-confidence to take a risk or develop a new skill. Some of us may need to crawl before we walk, while others may need to just take a leap and trust in yourself and those who support you.

I'll close this chapter on our money dysfunctions by saying this: I'm a second-generation veterinarian. My father grew up on a dairy farm and was the first of his family to go to college and then on to veterinary school on a 4-H scholarship. By all expectations at the time, he was to go back home and be the local vet while carrying on with the farm. Instead, he went into small animal practice briefly before taking the leap back to university for a PhD in anatomy. He then enjoyed a career in academia, which included another leap to becoming the dean of a veterinary school. His final career leap was into the pharmaceutical industry. All rewarding and all based on hard work, an openness to risk, and the pursuit of opportunity.

The more specific point about being in the driver's seat (and our focus in the upcoming chapters) is this: we must do what it takes to build passive income cash flow streams to become prosperous. This requires assuming some risk and delayed gratification, and that starts with shifting our mindset from working *for* money to making money *work for us*.

CHAPTER 3

WHAT IS PROSPERITY, ANYWAY?

By Andy Anderson

"Being *prosperous* is not having to think about money." That's a great line that I first heard from Dr. T, a veterinarian based in the southeastern US. Dr. T grew up on a dairy farm where hard work was the key to a successful life. This carried over to his development as a talented athlete, where the combination of raw talent and a strong work ethic produced powerful outcomes.

When it came to money, financial success was respected so long as one remained humble and made a reasonable effort to do some good with the gifts God had provided. Debt was to be avoided, as previous generations had encountered the pain of "owing the bank".

As a teenager, Dr. T identified his interest in healthcare and more specifically animals. His realization that he wanted to be a veterinarian was not met with enthusiasm by his father. With so much talent, his father wondered why he wouldn't become a physician, a path sure to yield a better financial outcome? This friction led to some degree of estrangement as Dr. T went down the path of his veterinary education and entrepreneurship in building a successful multi-doctor practice. His practice ultimately grew to be worth several million dollars when sold.

> **His father wondered why he wouldn't become a physician, a path sure to yield a better financial outcome?**

In interviewing Dr. T for this book, he remarked to me that, looking back on his path to success, at no time was making money the primary driver of starting his practice. Rather he sought to create a unique environment for people to work in while providing excellent, state of the art, veterinary care.

Importantly, Dr. T recognized the practice's value was created by the contributions of many and was a first derivative of the Purpose of his work. In other words, the practice's *Purpose* (and that of everyone within it) was the driving force of its success. I likewise have found through experience that "Purpose leads financial returns" to be a universal truth.

People often say, "Do what you love and the rest will take care of itself." This is a half-truth. A better saying would be, "Do what you love in a financially viable way and the rest will take care of itself." For Dr. T, this meant that at the time of his sale, he shared a significant portion of the proceeds with his long-term employees and colleagues.

Dr. T remains somewhat uncomfortable with his wealth and continues to invest it in projects that both do "good" and produce a financial return. He insists that his investments lead with the heart and not the wallet. Dr. T has the unique ability to find projects in real estate and other realms that meet his high and somewhat uncommon underwriting standards. For example, he is currently developing a diverse, sustainable mixed use (commercial and residential) property focused on the arts and a healthy lifestyle.

Through his financial freedom and prosperity, he has uncovered his passion for expression through art. He has become a prolific artist and is beginning to sell his work to collectors and friends. He's continuing to lead with his passion while also building assets and doing good.

Dr. T is able to live his life of fulfillment and make decisions without thinking first about money—and that's real prosperity. But how do we get there? From Dr. T's story—and that of hundreds of veterinarians I've worked with, including myself—I see the destination of comprehensive prosperity as arising from our journey on three related paths: those of purpose, work, and freedom.

Purpose, Work, and Freedom

> "Work is Love made visible"
> **KAHLIL GIBRAN**

As we are in pursuit of *prosperity*, we should have a common understanding of what it might look like if we catch it.

Dr. T's definition, "being prosperous is not having to think about money," provides a starting point. But his has no dollar amount attached, is based on the needs of an individual, and is highly variable. So let's dig deeper and see if there's a more accurate definition – or even a formula – for prosperity.

In the age of AI, who could resist interrogating ChatGPT on the question of "what is prosperity, anyway?" Its answer: "Prosperity refers to a state of thriving, abundance, and success in various aspects of life, such as financial wealth, personal well-being, social progress, and overall flourishing. It implies the presence of favorable circumstances, opportunities for growth, and the attainment of goals, leading to a high standard of living and overall satisfaction."

That's a great description of what I call **comprehensive prosperity**. Within it are some incontrovertible attributes on which we can agree. First, prosperity is best thought of in *Financial* and *Non-Financial* terms.

Financial Prosperity
+ Non-Financial Prosperity
= Total Prosperity

The financial goal for some might simply be the ability to cover the basic costs of life in retirement with the help of Social Security payments and Medicare. Others want the resources to pursue some activity at a particular age plus take care of the basics. Travel; rock climb; snow ski 100 days a year; become an artist; retrain as a minister; these are all examples of goals I've heard other vets declare when thinking of what their wealth needs to fund.

The best of all worlds is when we have prosperity-building work that aligns with our Purpose—the reason we get up every morning. (As I've said, my Purpose is to *Learn, Share, and Serve*.)

We all need to be productive, to love and to be loved, and to have aspirations and hopes. Simon Sinek describes the underpinning of this concept for organizations as their *Why* and comments that we are defined not by *what* we do but *why* we do it.[7]

Veterinarians, thankfully, are blessed to have the obvious Purpose of serving their patients and clients. This is a perfect start to the process of defining your own *Purpose*. (While the topic of discovering one's Purpose is beyond the limited scope of this book, I am personally fond of Richard Leider's insights in his books, *The Power of Purpose: Find Meaning, Live Longer, Better* and *Who Do You Want to Be When You Grow Old?: The Path of Purposeful Aging*, among others.)

The point is we must not discount the importance of Purpose. It's an underappreciated but essential component of

---

[7] Sinek, Simon. 2009. *Start With Why: How Great Leaders Inspire Everyone to Take Action.* http://ci.nii.ac.jp/ncid/BB07258461.

our health, wealth, and happiness. Professor Victor Strecher, a celebrated researcher of purpose and the author of *Life on Purpose*, wrote this about his discoveries:

> "Let's imagine a drug that was shown to add years to your life; reduce the risk of heart attack and stroke; cut your risk of Alzheimer's disease by more than half; help you relax during the day and sleep better at night; double your chances of staying drug- and alcohol-free after treatment; activate your natural killer cells; diminish your inflammatory cells; increase your good cholesterol; and repair your DNA. What if this imaginary drug reduced hospital stays so much that it put a dent in the national health-care crisis? Oh, and as a bonus, gave you better sex? The pharmaceutical company who made the drug would be worth billions. The inventors of the drug would receive Nobel Prizes and have institutes named for them! But it's not a drug. It's **Purpose**. And it's free."[8]

I placed Kahlil Gibran's wonderful quote from *The Prophet* at the top of this subchapter for good reason. I believe "work" is our greatest opportunity to practice love beyond our immediate family. It's a platform for us to demonstrate care with deep kindness and love for the animals and people we encounter. The work is far more important to us than the money. It is an act of purposeful service to others. It is the principle-defining

---

[8] Strecher, Victor J. 2016. *Life on Purpose: How Living for What Matters Most Changes Everything*. HarperCollins.

activity of our expression of love. I personally believe work is what we were built for by God. It facilitates our adult journey to favorable circumstances, opportunities for growth, and the attainment of goals, leading to a high standard of living and overall satisfaction.

Today, as a society and as a profession, we are questioning the benefits of work. In some cases, there's the suggestion that somehow our work should be *subordinated* to a host of other things. This "work-life balance" trend is interestingly accompanied by the corresponding decline in faith activities, the nuclear family, and the number of in-person friends and community interactions. At the same time, the overall suicide rates in our country have increased 30 percent in the first two decades of this century, to the point where 5 percent of Americans adults have reported serious thoughts of suicide.[9] Alcoholism, drug abuse, use of antidepressants, and more are all growing at alarming rates.

We are living longer and longer. Healthcare, pharmaceuticals (think statins and now GLP-1 drugs) and our conscious decisions about our physical health and aging are significantly impacting our life span. Even more important than lifespan is *"healthspan."* Healthspan is that period where our health does not impair our ability to be active and enjoy the pursuits we choose. I would suggest healthspan is more important than lifespan and that our goal should be to have healthspan equal lifespan.

9 "Suicide." 2021. National Institute of Mental Health (NIMH). 2021. https://www.nimh.nih.gov/health/statistics/suicide.

Financial freedom expands what is possible for how we execute our Purpose by eliminating a financial outcome as a significant driver of our decisions. Some might consider financial wealth or freedom may be reached at a point where passive income funds 50 percent or 75 percent of your needs—then, when combined with some income from work and other sources, the "lines cross."

> **Financial freedom expands what is possible for how we execute our Purpose by eliminating a financial outcome as a significant driver of our decisions.**

You can easily be productive well into your seventies or even eighties. You may not be a busy clinician seeing twenty-five patients a day, but there are many opportunities in our profession for work deceleration into part-time roles. The concept of leaving the profession when you are among the wisest, most mature clinicians is disastrous for younger veterinarians. We lose out not only on your productivity but also on your experience, wisdom, and mentorship.

Even worse is when highly skilled young veterinarians significantly downsize their commitment to work or leave the profession completely. Lost is their manifestation of their training and collective mentorship and knowledge acquired through all their education.

As a profession, we have gone from working 6 days a week, to 5 days, to 4 days or less. Are we becoming a part-time profession? Should we assume that we can maintain our historical authority and admiration in our communities as part-timers? If "practice" is what we do to get better, are we getting as much "practice" as we need?

This is where Purpose is most essential. I believe the principle of working with Purpose is our expression of God's love and the antidote to much of today's malaise. When combined with building the non-financial components of prosperity and happiness – family, faith, in-person friendships, and health – this type of committed work is transformative and curative. I encourage you to approach all these topics more exhaustively in *Full-Time: Work and the Meaning of Life* by David L. Bahnsen (a clear thinker and wonderfully honest writer who happens to be a committed dividend investor).

Recently, a Dr. PK told me this about his path to veterinary medicine. He grew up on a farm and recounted that when things went wrong with a cow or a horse, it was a family emergency. The family was stressed. The vet was called. He remembers when the vet's truck came down the lane, everyone had a feeling that "things were going to be okay." He identified that he wanted to be that person. He wanted to serve others and have that feeling of "earned success." Talk about Purpose!

Arthur Brooks brought us the idea of "earned success," which highlights the psychic rewards of work. It captures the inner feeling of not just *receiving* something, but *earning* it, which meaningfully forms the basis for self-worth and deserved recognition. Importantly, earned success is achieved through the service of others, not from a vanity-based serving of oneself. The basic economic reality at the heart of "earned success" is that we become valuable in the marketplace (and achieve this inner satisfaction) only when we are *valuable to others through our services and work.*

YOUR ONE-OF-A-KIND IMPACT

The rotary phone on the bedside table rang at 2 am. It was the fall of 1957. A woman had presented to the emergency department with acute abdominal pain. Diagnostics and her clinical picture were consistent with a ruptured appendix. The on-call surgeon dutifully answered the phone, listened to the case's facts, and shuffled off to get dressed. Duty called. For him it was the work and his expression of his God given talents he had signed up for when entering medical school.

I owe my life to this unknown surgeon who answered the call and did his job thoroughly, professionally, and completely. Let me explain. All of you know that the first rule of having a body cavity open is to do a "complete exploratory." I like to do it before I address the known problems when my eyes are fresh. That's exactly what he did and, low and behold, in addition to the ruptured appendix, his patient, my mother, had a large ovarian tumor. He solved both problems by doing his job, even at 4 AM.

It turns out my mother's reproductive status was completely out of whack due to the tumor's production of hormones. She had been unable to conceive for nine years and had virtually given up on a second child. Well, three months later, morning sickness arrived, and six months after that, I was born. Fortunately, the tumor was benign.

If you have ever watched the Jimmy Stewart classic, *It's a Wonderful Life*, you know the story winds its way through a life that ends up in despair and on the brink of suicide due to financial ruin. Angels save the day by creating a vision for Stewart's character, George Bailey, of what his community would have been like without him and the work he did. The vision helped him realize how "wonderful" his life had been and how much good he had done. This vision led him back to his family and gratitude.

George Bailey could never have known these truths without divine intervention, and neither can we. But we can imagine the unseen results of our good works, small encouragements, mentorship, and leadership in the world. Know this—without your one-of-kind impact, so many things would not be as wonderful as they are today. It is a reason to have Purpose and touch as many people as possible and to be grateful for your work.

One day, I hope I can say thank you to that surgeon for answering the rotary phone and doing the work God had given him to do, and I hope he is well pleased with what I have done with the life that he enabled in that OR in 1957.

I will continue to try to live up to the opportunity I've been given.

Prosperity Is Not Just About Money

One of my mentors, Gordon Cain, had a wonderful corporate career. He was an army officer, chemical engineer, and chemical executive for many years. When we met, he was 71 and had a net worth of about $1.5 million with some passive income. He led a comfortable but not extravagant life. He loved to work, help others, and empower leaders and organizations to grow.

I worked with Gordon and his partner Frank Hevrdejs for several years acquiring over 25 businesses. In fact, this was the last stop of my finance career. My next stop? Veterinary school. Gordon continued to be active in business well into his 80s.

By the time Gordon passed away (still working), he had been inducted into the Texas Business Hall of Fame, had a net worth of hundreds of millions of dollars, had funded all sorts of philanthropic activities, and was surrounded by those he loved. Gordon didn't need his wealth to fund a big life transition to doing nothing and focusing on consumption. (Although his wife made him stop driving his 15-year-old Oldsmobile 88 and buy a Mercedes.) He loved what he did and pursued his passion and Purpose—prosperity was simply a byproduct.

I frequently hear from aging veterinarians that they still love to practice but there is just too much work to do. They need to work less and at the same time, like Gordon, continue in their profession.

I have a friend, Dr. JC, a veterinarian in the Midwest, who was supremely successful and got the "lines to cross" and then some through practice ownership, real estate investing, and dividend paying stocks.

JC was raised in the home of a dedicated pediatrician. He joined his father on hospital rounds frequently and saw medicine up close and personal in the neonatal units of a major east coast city. His father was Purpose-driven and was completely dedicated to his practice and family.

Fascinated with life science and animals, JC can't remember a time when he didn't want to be a veterinarian (a familiar story for so many of us). At this time in the 1970s and 1980s, veterinarians were known as happy, fulfilled, and engaged—"some of the happiest professionals I knew," says JC. "They weren't yet the indebted, depressed, and on-suicide-watch cohort we know today."

JC's family narrative on money ("money script") was the "pursuit of the American Dream." Work hard, do the right thing, build, save, invest, and create a better life for the next generation. JC's family was financially comfortable and making progress, neither money-driven nor money averse. They believed success could and would be theirs. And JC continued that path to great success.

In addition to his practice, JC invested well in income producing real estate, farmland, and dividend paying stocks. His financial freedom and well-deserved prosperity are making a positive impact on his mentees, students, and numerous charitable organizations.

Now in his 60's after a brief "retirement," he is back to practicing and teaching what he loves, only now at the right dose. His other time goes to support his wife (who has health challenges) and his children and grandchildren.

Without his wealth, JC could be burdened by stifling healthcare costs and needing to work harder and longer than would be healthy for him and his family. JC's financial success has provided far better healthcare than insurance could provide and the ability to sleep well at night knowing that his wife will have the care she needs without regard to cost.

"Prosperity is not just money," says JC. "It includes so many things including the ability to provide for your children and grandchildren. Things like capital to start a business, pay for education, take care of those in need, and give back to your community."

When I asked JC about his approach to prosperity, he said this: "We never set out to be wealthy, we just worked our asses off, took care of patients and people, and did the right thing—and the success came."

> **We never set out to be wealthy, we just worked our asses off, took care of patients and people, and did the right thing—and the success came.**

A Life Well-Lived

Life is a portfolio of things, relationships, and experiences, with *things* being the least important. Eckhart Tolle cleverly reminds us in *A New Earth* that as we approach death, the whole concept of "ownership" stands revealed as ultimately *meaningless*. When all is said and done, we are all just passing through and are only stewards of the things to which we mistakenly claim ownership.

Being comprehensively prosperous requires a balance of the financial and the non-financial. Wealth provides time to play, create, give, exercise, think, and experience. Where "work-life balance" truly misses the point is in its erroneous duality. The thing that balances work is not life but play or rest. Life, rather, is the totality of God's gift to us. Work, rest, and play are just parts of life. (God provided the 6:1 ratio between work and rest to get us on the right track. "On the seventh day he rested.")

I fully support dating, marriage, children, vacations, play, friendships, naps and whatever else is part of building a complete and balanced, well-lived life. One should not objectify or idolize any component of life, including work or money. Workaholism is bad. Social comparison, as Teddy Roosevelt said long before Instagram, is the "thief of joy." How much misery could be removed from society if we didn't pursue constant comparison to others through social media?

Work is not set against life and is not the underlying problem. Work is a significant part of our experience and is our path to "earned success" and being something of value to others, ourselves, and society.

My hope is that if you believe work is causing you stress and mental illness, do not fall into the trap of *blaming* your profession or employer. As we explore later in the book, you are in control of how you respond to any stimulus. Doing *less* work will not make you happy. Thinking differently about work and integrating it into a complete life, will. Work falls into place when it's merely a component of prosperity and *happier*ness (Oprah Winfrey's word).

I have had a close relationship to one of the most beautiful mountain towns in North America. I've known the town's leaders and first responders and listened to their accounts of the drug-related emergencies and suicides—which, sadly, are off the charts. When describing the situation, one paramedic told me, "It's always the same story—people who are struggling emotionally reposition themselves for play in a beautiful place thinking fun and beauty will fix them." As someone who has been depressed and anxious, let me tell you, changing our setting usually doesn't overcome our issues. Only internal change does this. (Get help from a mental health professional!) As my mother loved to say, "Bloom where you are planted!" Plus, the outcomes are always better when we make big changes and big decisions when we are healthy.

By expanding the definition of prosperity and happierness to include the *non-financial* components (mental and physical health, family, fun, community, giving, faith, and friends), we create a more complete picture of a prosperous, well-lived life that was funded by our work and investing activities.

We often struggle measuring the value of *non-financial* components of prosperity. Let me assure you, that while not dependent on money, they are easier to achieve with resources and ultimately far more valuable. Later, in Chapters 9 and 10, we'll discuss some tools to help create a Life Plan, to chart your journey to building comprehensive prosperity, *happier*ness, and the life you envision and control.

But first, let's wrap up the fundamentals by covering a few universal principles of money.

CHAPTER 4

THE PRINCIPLES OF MONEY

By Andy Anderson and Brent Mayabb

AA Dr. John is married to a talented veterinarian who joined our practice, and I got to know him through our friendship. While John was working in a great practice, he often considered going out on his own. I and others encouraged John for over three years, pushing him to take the leap. He was hesitant due to the risks and costs involved. While it was clear to me that he had great potential, like my father, his risk aversion was holding him back.

A big part of our risk aversion is our lack of familiarity with the fundamentals of money. We avoid concepts like compound interest, leverage, time value of money, value of cash flow, and dividend-paying investments, among others, because they are foreign to us. But once we familiarize ourselves with some of money's basic principles, suddenly any perceived "risk" becomes smaller.

After three years of encouraging John to start his own practice, we had a conversation about the principles of money. It was helpful for him to see how certain timeless principles could be applied to his situation to mitigate risk. During our discussion of dividend-paying investments and concepts such as compounding, leverage, and cash flow valuations, something clicked for him. He especially appreciated dividend-paying investments because they provided tangible cash returns every quarter.

Finally convinced, he took a risk and started his own practice, which became very successful. Later, we ended up becoming partners, and John was able to achieve early financial freedom. He retained 25-30 percent ownership and later opened another practice with us.

It should be said that John and his wife are exceptional individuals. She is a high-earning veterinarian to whom Fred and I "gifted" equity in our first business due to her massive contributions. John is a diligent and successful veterinarian owning two practices. They are complete overachievers, demonstrating what it looks like when you do things perfectly.

What I like about Dr. John's story is that once he got comfortable with the basics, and learned how to calculate risk, he didn't stop there. His brother, a lawyer, provided terrific support, and together they went into some more advanced territory, such as investing in commercial real estate and other non-veterinary businesses. John then used the proceeds from selling part of his first practice to invest in a dividend growth strategy, while his command of the basics gave him confidence to eventually pursue *all three* paths to financial prosperity (more on dividends and the paths to wealth in Chapter 5).

Today, John and his family are living in the southwest, building wealth, enjoying family life, and living well. They are achieving financial freedom. While they might not declare victory just yet, they are doing exceptionally well. They have wonderful children and some fun consumption spending, so they want to continue building prosperity. They love the process of growing, are now comfortable with the principles of money, and are in a great spot to achieve comprehensive prosperity.

For many veterinarians, the principles of money seem like alchemy. They aren't. They are not even a well-guarded secret. They just appear to be because most of us don't approach them at an early age.

Money has a language of its own and just like the language of veterinary medicine, it requires some thoughtful study to obtain mastery. Most people wouldn't understand our terminology like Panel, U/A, R&A, or TECA. Similarly, financial terms seem foreign until we spend time learning their language. We've isolated a few of the key principles here and expanded on them for your benefit:

- compound interest
- time value of money
- leverage
- asset valuation of cash flow.

An understanding of these principles will allow you to make fast progress toward building prosperity.

As you will know from your personal finance course (that we recommended in Chapter 2), the table stakes of building wealth include the disciplines of budgeting, savings, debt management, insurance, estate planning, and building a financial plan. The principles we discuss here are a layer deeper and compose the mechanism of action for capital formation.

Importantly, these tenants of money are very closely related. I asked our colleague, Brent Mayabb, DVM, MS, to address the compound interest topic. Brent is a terrific example of how a veterinarian can save and invest wisely.

THE MAGIC OF COMPOUND INTEREST

BM I did not grow up around money, nor around people who knew how to manage it. I was the first person in my family to attend college and the first to earn a doctorate. There was no roadmap for financial success in my family or even among my close circle of friends.

While in veterinary school, a prevailing narrative suggested that becoming a veterinarian was *not* a route to wealth. It was almost as if they were preparing us for a life of modest means. Even though I didn't choose this profession to become wealthy, I also didn't believe that choosing to become a veterinarian should condemn me to poverty. Believing otherwise, I took out student loans. By the time I graduated, my debt was two and a quarter times my initial salary, which was a crushing burden—it felt like paying for a house without having a place to live. Would it ever get easier?

While working my first year in practice, a more experienced veterinarian pulled me aside one evening. "Has anybody ever talked to you about retirement?"

I blinked, not quite understanding.

"You're going to need money saved up in order to live. Do you do have a plan?"

I did not. The concept was so completely foreign to me that it had never even crossed my mind.

Using a photocopy of an article from a financial magazine, the older veterinarian proceeded to explain the concept to me, pointing regularly to a chart showing the potential growth of investing $2,000 annually in a Roth IRA and an S&P 500 account starting in one's twenties. By retirement at age 65, this could accumulate to over a million dollars.

I was skeptical about becoming a millionaire, but he clarified that it was about retirement savings and the power of *compound interest*. As we walked through the financial plan, I realized, "Oh my gosh, this works. Holy cow!" (While investing in a mutual fund does not guarantee returns, it's highly likely to yield results over time.)

This conversation marked the beginning of my passion for personal finance. He was merely trying to help a colleague, spending a few hours guiding a younger person in need. What he didn't anticipate was igniting my enduring interest in the subject. I started devouring books on personal finance, realizing the truth in his advice about retirement savings and recognizing its applicability to other financial areas beyond tax-advantaged accounts.

Later, I switched jobs to one that offered an employer match for the Simple IRA and eventually a 401(k). I maximized all my retirement contributions and also invested in a non-taxable account. During the late 1990s and early 2000s, I watched my balances grow each month, which was incredibly satisfying.

At that time, tech stocks were soaring, and it seemed like they would only continue to rise. Although I was tempted, I was always conservative with my money, keeping my retirement savings in mutual funds and only dabbling in individual stocks with extra cash. This strategy paid off when the tech bubble burst; while individual stocks plummeted, my mutual funds experienced smaller losses. This was a valuable lesson in risk-adjusted returns. The stocks were exhilarating while they soared, but the mutual funds provided a more stable investment.

The financial challenges discussed by Andy, Chip, and Jen throughout *The Prosperous Veterinarian* remain widespread. The difference between when I experienced these issues and today is the general awareness. More people nowadays understand the need to address the financial challenges of our profession, whereas previously, the common solution was simply to buy a practice—a path I knew was *not* for me.

A significant aspect of being a prosperous veterinarian is recognizing the alternative paths available *aside* from owning a practice. I realized during vet school that I didn't want to pursue traditional veterinary practice—a decision that is quite uncommon. Interestingly, this realization deepened during an after-hours emergency surgery rotation with Dr. Andy Anderson, a resident at the time who had a background in finance. While assisting him in surgery, I shared my career uncertainty—torn between a business-oriented path and going into research.

Dr. Anderson casually remarked that I seemed more suited for the business track. Although it might have been a passing comment for him, to me, it was validation from someone who had succeeded in business. This conversation sparked my interest in exploring opportunities in the business side of veterinary medicine, such as working for a pharmaceutical company. Soon after, I spoke with industry professionals, who recommended I first get practice experience for three to five years to understand the customer's perspective.

Following their advice, I spent three years in practice before sending out my CV. By the fifth year, I transitioned into the pet food industry, where I continue to work today.

By the seventh year, I had paid off my student loans. Around the same time, I got married to a fellow veterinarian who, fortunately, had no debt. Within eight years of purchasing our home, we managed to pay off the mortgage, largely due to the compounding effect and having extra money from our investments.

For the first decade of our journey, my wife and I lived *very* frugally. We survived on my salary alone and used her earnings to aggressively pay down my student loans.

After clearing the loans, we then directed her income towards accelerating our mortgage payments.

Shortly after achieving these milestones, my wife and I reached financial freedom. There's a lot of debate about the precise figures needed for financial freedom, but for me, it means being able to live comfortably on the returns from my investments without needing to work. (That being said, I still enjoy my work, and for now choose to reinvest all returns back into the principal.)

I should call out that perhaps the most pivotal (and stone simple) aspect of my financial success was *automating* my investments. Every payday, the money I had designated for mutual funds was directly debited from my paycheck account. This simple automation was critical because, without it, I likely wouldn't have made a single contribution!

It's been over 25 years since I had the first conversation about retirement back in 1998. Today, I can affirm that the math checks out—the principles of compound interest have held true, just as illustrated in the magazine article my mentor once showed me. Despite the usual fluctuations of markets, the financial forecasts have proven amazingly accurate.

Over the past decade, as personal finance and investing became my passion, I've strived to develop my expertise further. Recognizing that most veterinarians aren't keen on financial matters, I decided to use my ability to 'speak both languages' to make finance more accessible to them.

At the age of 50, I returned to school to earn a master's degree in financial planning—not to become a practicing financial planner, but to educate and empower other veterinarians. Now, I speak at meetings, schools, and conferences. My goal is to demystify money management and make it more approachable, not only for young veterinarians, but also for those in mid or late careers who may not have a solid financial plan.

Late-career vets, particularly those who own practices, face unique challenges as they prepare to sell their practices and lose their regular salary and dividends. My aim is to help them navigate these changes effectively. In many ways, the journey, for me, has come full circle.

There have been countless great memories along the way, but perhaps the best is the initial realization that our financial strategy was working. About 14 years into our journey, in 2012, during a conversation with my father-in-law on our back porch, he asked a question similar to the one the older veterinarian asked me at the beginning of my journey: "What's your retirement plan?"

I told him we had about $500,000 already saved for retirement.

"You mean $50,000?" he asked.

"No," I said. "Five *hundred* thousand."

He about near fell out of his chair! As much he was initially shocked, I know he felt a great deal of relief. There was no need to worry about the future of his daughter and son-in-law. Thanks to a little knowledge, thriftiness, and the magic of compound interest, we were going to be all right.

Compound Interest

As Brent likes to say, Albert Einstein is often credited with saying, "Compound interest is the eighth wonder of the world." Why would a theoretical physicist, and one of the most influential scientists of all time, make such a definitive statement about a financial topic, of all things? Clearly, the compounding of money must be important!

Compounding occurs when the returns on your investment are *reinvested* and added to the principal (what you started with) to generate even more returns. In other words, *your earnings make money on top of your beginning principal*, and your returns become exponential instead of linear over time.

To illustrate this, let's look at a simple example with two vets. Dr. Nick wants to invest his money and take his returns and use them to buy things he wants in the present. Dr. Laura wants to invest to grow her wealth for the future by taking advantage of compounding.

They both have $10,000 to start with and plan to invest 15 percent of their pre-tax salary of $150,000 every month. They will make this investment into a tax deferred account like a 401(k). They both use an investment approach that makes a 7 percent return, paid annually. After year one, the math on the investment return for Nick and Laura is the same, and it looks like this:

Return = principal X rate of return X time
Return = $10,000 X 7% X 1 year
Return = $700

Moving forward, Nick takes his return ($700) and spends it, so his principal remains the same at $10,000 plus the $22,500 he invests every year. So, in year two, the return is calculated exactly the same as above, except the principal is now $32,500: Nick earns $2,275 in year 2. Nick can buy more stuff!

For Laura, compounding begins in year two. Her $700 return from year one gets added to the principal ($10,700), plus her next year savings of $22, 500 making it $33,200. So, in year two, her return increases:

$33,200 X 7% X 1 year = $2,324
Beginning year 3 her account is $33,200* + $2,324 = $35,324

*I've simplified the calculation to assume this year's savings was invested at the beginning of the year.

Poor Laura, she was so disciplined, and she deprived herself of buying stuff and having fun only to be $3,000 ahead of Nick after two years. But let's not judge Laura prematurely. If we run this scenario forward twenty-five years, here is what we see:

At the end of twenty-five years, Laura has $1,477,377 in her account, while Nick has $572,500.

Laura's discipline has been rewarded by racking up $904,877 more than Nick. With the assumptions held constant, Laura's account will be throwing off $103,000 in year 25 while Nick only has $40,000 to spend.

This difference illustrates the critical impact of time on compounding! The longer it goes, the more rapidly the total value grows in the later years. Changing the other factors such as increasing the rate of return or the amount of the investment will also increase the future value, but sometimes our current situations do not allow us to impact those variables dramatically. But if we invest, like Laura, then we can allow *time* to do its work and see similar returns.

Einstein was right about the wonder of compounding, and unlike the Seven Wonders of the Ancient World, it's right here waiting for any of us to use it in dividend paying stocks, real estate, and practice ownership. The earlier you start, the better the outcome. The most valuable dollar you save is the first one. Get started today!

Time Value of Money

The concept of the *time value of money* is a corollary to compounding. I like to illustrate this concept with the following question: *Would you prefer to receive $1,000 today ("present value") or $1,000 one year from now ("future value")?*

Most would answer $1,000 now and assign the reasoning to something like, "Well, a bird in the hand…" or "I'm not sure you'll be around in a year." All good points, but the financial truth is that you want the money *now* because you can invest it and in one year (assuming a 7% return) have $1,070 or more in one year depending upon how often the investment pays a return that you can reinvest and compound.

Let's keep it simple and say it only pays out its return at the end of the one-year period, which is called "Simple Interest".

Now let's ask a slightly more complicated question: Would you prefer $1,000 today or $1,400 in 7 years?

Oh boy, that is a little tougher.

If you immediately said, obviously $1,400 in 7 years, let's take a closer look. To get at the right answer you have to decide at what rate of return you could invest the $1,000 today for the next seven years.

Let's say you know you can earn 7 percent per year on your money. Oops. You lost $205 by jumping the gun and taking the $1400 in 7 years. Investing $1,000 for 7 years at a 7% return would have given you $1,605. Said another way, your decision to take the $1400 implied that you could only earn about 5 percent on the money. Even worse, if you could have invested the principal at a 9 percent rate of return, the total value would have been over $1,800.

These examples indicate how financial decisions are highly dependent upon time horizons and expectation of returns. They are like wagers or bets, where our ability to accurately predict probabilities will influence our cumulative outcome.

Another way to approach the exercise is the following example: Let's say you had a friend who won the lottery and knew that he would receive $1.0 million per year for 10 years ($10 million total). But he really wanted to do something special with some of the money today and wanted to sell you today the 10th installment of $1.0 million that he was going to receive in 10 years.

In other words, you would get (for certain) $1.0 million ten years from today but you had to pay for it. What would you pay? It helps if you make a guess before we do the math together. Fill in your guess: _____.

The $1.0 million, 10 years out, is the Future Value. The price we would be willing to pay today is the Present Value. Let's assume that you had the money to purchase the Future Payment. You would have to decide what return you could earn on that money to help arrive at the "price" you would pay today for the $1.0 million future payment in 10 years.

Assume that you would be happy with a 10 percent return in this case. Accordingly, you should be willing to pay *only $385,543* for the right to receive $1.0 million in 10 years. In other words, the $385,543 will compound in 10 years to be $1 million. (And the higher your assumed target rate of return, the less you would be willing to pay today. Try using the calculator we recommended at a 5 percent and 15 percent assumed return.)

Surprised? These concepts should become integrated into your thinking when dealing with financial decisions. Keep asking yourself: *How would the time value of money principle apply to this decision?*

Keep asking yourself: *How would the time value of money principle apply to this decision?*

Leverage

"Leverage" is the word financially sophisticated people use for debt or borrowed money. The term extends the concept of mechanical leverage, which is the use of simple machines or levers to amplify forces to enable more work or weight to be moved. Financial leverage refers to using borrowed money strategically to enhance the potential return on an investment. The use of leverage or debt also amplifies risk because of the obligations to make timely repayments of principal and interest.

When considering an investment, you must account for the business risks of the investment—and if debt is employed, the financial risks of the use of leverage. Accordingly, always remember the risk of an investment or business may be thought in terms of the formula:

Business Risk + Financial Risk = Total Risk

You are using leverage in your life if you have student loans, car loans, credit card debt, or a home mortgage. The concept is quite simple. You are renting someone else's capital with the promise to pay it back plus the rent or interest payments. Your work and paycheck have become the source of compounding for the lender. The details of the contract are very important, but the application of the principles of compounding and the time value of money to the concept of leverage is foundational.

Let's look at your student loan. If you borrowed $250,000 for your veterinary education, you will need to earn (using the asset you bought with the loan, a DVM degree) a sufficient income to not only pay your living expenses, save for a rainy day, and fund your investment capital, but also to repay part of the principal of the loan plus the interest every year.

If the interest rate or rent is 5 percent on your student loan, you must deploy the loan's capital in a way that produces a return in excess of 5 percent annually plus the annual portion of $250,000 you originally borrowed for this to be a good decision for you. If the loan is to be repaid in fifteen years, then you will need to earn $23,550 per year to meet this obligation. Let's say you earn $150,000 per year. Your debt service requirement is roughly 9.5 percent of your income on a pre-tax basis and 22 percent-plus of your after-tax cash.

Please pay very close attention to the state in which you choose to live as it relates to your after-tax earnings. If you choose to live in CA, NY, or other high state income tax jurisdictions, then you will have to earn much higher compensation to keep up with your colleagues in low tax states. (You can use a free calculator online to help you with this analysis for different scenarios.)[10]

> **Please pay very close attention to the state in which you choose to live as it relates to your after-tax earnings.**

---

10 https://www.bankrate.com or https://www.calculator.net/

As a comparison, let's look at a typical industrial business making an equipment investment. This business might use the same $250,000 you borrowed to purchase new machinery, and they would plan for the investment to earn at least 15-20 percent cash flow annually after all debt service (the $23,550) and expenses were paid. Let's say about $40,000 per year that could be reinvested in a compounding way. To maintain the equivalent economics, you would have to save and invest $40,000 per year or 27 percent of your $150,000 income. This would be very unlikely based on my experience.

Applying the same logic and comparing the machinery investment with your veterinary degree, we might find that the veterinary degree was an inferior investment. But why? Is it because you are undisciplined in controlling your expenses? Or have you not been successful at generating enough income from the assets (your degrees) you command? Of course, it is ridiculous to compare a machinery investment to a veterinary degree—but it is enlightening.

Valuation of Cash Flow

Cash flow streams are remarkable in the sense that investors will pay *multiples* of the annual dollars received from an asset. The multiple applied by a buyer of a cash-flow producing asset is influenced by many factors.

Let's examine those factors through the example of a veterinary practice. The table below shows factors affecting the cash flow valuation multiple for a hypothetical veterinary practice and the direction of its impact.

Table 1: Practice Characteristics and Impact on Valuation

Multiple veterinarians with owner production less than 20% of total revenue	↑ (INCREASE)
Room for expansion on property	↑ (INCREASE)
Profit margin of 16% or greater	↑ (INCREASE)
Revenue growing at 3% per year	↓ (DECREASE)
Mature area that is not adding new homes/patients	↓ (DECREASE)

Ultimately the cash flow produced by a business goes to the owners of all the claims against the business. These include suppliers, lenders, and equity owners. We must assume that the valuation of an asset or business arrived at by applying a multiple of cash flow must somehow satisfy all the claims on the business. This total value is known as Enterprise Value. The value left over after all the claims are satisfied is the Equity Value, which is the property of the owners of the practice.

Buyers focus on the *cash flow stream* after allowance for expenses needed to keep the stream healthy and growing. Things like investments in replacing equipment or repairing facilities are examples of recurring expenses without which the cash flow stream would slow down or even dry up. This modified cash flow is known as Free Cash Flow, since it is available or "free" to be used by the owner for other purposes without harming the business.

Bottomline: These principles of money are the building blocks of thinking through the financial impact of your decisions. To put a finer point on it: they are the guiding truths behind how the businesses you interact with think about *you* as their counter-party. For instance, this is how your bank, Zoetis, IDEXX, and your landlord think about their money. Understanding the principles of money puts you on equal footing with those you do business with and provides you insight into how to conduct your relationships. Use them wisely and often!

Understanding the principles of money puts you on equal footing with those you do business with and provides you insight into how to conduct your relationships.

CHAPTER 5

THREE PREDICTABLE PATHS TO FINANCIAL PROSPERITY

By Andy Anderson, Jennifer Welser, and Chip Cannon

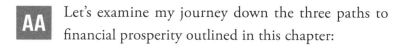 Let's examine my journey down the three paths to financial prosperity outlined in this chapter:

→ Dividend-paying investments
→ Practice ownership
→ Real estate ventures

For me, dividend-paying investments happened first. These investments functioned basically like savings, allowing for the accumulation of capital while compounding in *anticipation* of future opportunities (such as starting a practice or investing in real estate). Putting most of my "savings" into these regular taxable brokerage accounts, I didn't put too much into an IRA or 401(k), as these structures render the capital inaccessible (until age 59.5) for other investments (without having to pay an early withdrawal penalty).

I was introduced to dividend-paying investments in the 1980s and started investing in my early twenties. Over the years, I found that the average returns consistently outperformed inflation, safeguarding my money against devaluation (which can happen if you leave your cash under the mattress or keep it in a low-to-no interest checking or savings account). My portfolio returns over the past 15 years, for instance, compounded at around 10 percent with tolerable volatility. Yes, there were some sleepless nights and moments of hand-wringing, but the dividends kept coming in bad times and good, which helped me to weather the downturns.

I maintained my investments in dividend-paying accounts and reinvested the returns from the late 1980s until about 2000, during which time the capital continued to compound. Typically, veterinarians tend to transition to practice ownership in their late 30s to early 40s, after around 10 to 15 years of saving and professional development.

Despite the benefits of dividend-paying investments, I've noticed that few younger veterinarians invest in them. Sure, paying off debt is a big priority during these early years, which is one of the significant reasons younger professionals tend to save and invest so little. But even among those with a bit of surplus, most younger veterinarians I meet are typically investing in random strategies. While such approaches may yield reasonable returns over the long term, they are more volatile and lack the cash flow stream that helps veterinarians start building real wealth *today*.

Around 2000, I began moving towards practice ownership, the second predictable path to prosperity. Our first practice was a quick success. Reinvesting profits back into the business—such as upgrading to a larger, more specialized facility—fueled greater growth. Moreover, owning the real estate where the practice operated allowed us to leverage cash flows into additional investments, such as acquiring shopping centers—real estate being the third predictable path to prosperity.

By the age of 50, I achieved basic financial freedom, enabled by strategic pursuit of the three predictable paths to financial prosperity. Keep in mind, that once all the pieces of the picture came together, this goal only took ten to twelve years to achieve.

Before we go deeper into each path, please allow me a moment to share what I believe is the secret ingredient common to these three paths.

Pattern Recognition and the Cash-Flow Stream

Rivers and streams are vital natural resources to our ecosystems, providing the essential lifeblood of fresh water and a cleansing flow. They support our food systems, biosystems, and a myriad of life forces. They enrich our culture and play a significant role in natural history. They even support recreation as fisheries and their flows provide the energy for paddle boarding and kayaking. And yet the massive breadth of their contribution is rarely appreciated.

I'm a fly fisherman. I love the rhythm of the river, the beauty of trout, and the lifecycle of aquatic insects. There is nothing like the sweet, earthy, moist smell of a high desert stream. Fly fishing is a great illustrator of the power of observation and patience. It is also an amazing metaphor for life. Above all it forces one to develop keen pattern recognition.

What can the surface of the water and the flow around the boulder or through the riffle tell you about the likely presence of a trout beneath the surface?

"Read the water" and you develop a sense for the relationship of the elements in the picture. Such pattern recognition increases your success exponentially. When trout rise, they have given you their address. Is their "take" of the insect a sip, slurp, or gulp? Is it explosive or subtle? These are the clues to what insect they are eating and the clue to the fisher of which microscopic ball of feathers to serve up to "fool" the fish.

This skill of pattern recognition dramatically increases one's enjoyment as a fisherman. Application of this skill to your quest for financial independence and prosperity is essential to becoming the master of your time. By the way, it is exactly the skill you develop as you become an experienced clinician, getting to the essence of a case in the most efficient way.

There is another type of stream that is just as remarkable, the *Cash-Flow Stream(s) (CFS)*. The CFS is also vital to our ecosystem. They, too, support our food and shelter, educate our children, build families, fund charities, and so much more. Enterprise Value is primarily derived from *Cash Flow Streams*. Passive *CFS* come from our practices and businesses, real estate, dividend paying stocks, interest, and royalties. They make up most sources of available wealth acquisition to veterinarians. Other sources of wealth come from scarce asset appreciation or other stores of wealth such as collectibles, art, bitcoin, gold, and land.

The big takeaway: As you begin to see the patterns of CFS, you will increase your odds of success in becoming a part of their flows.

One amazing thing about cash flow streams is that they are valued as a multiple of their annual cash flow. An example is the $500,000 *CFS* from a practice may be assigned a value of 8 times, or $4.0 million. A high-quality piece of commercial real estate producing a $500,000 CFS may trade at 15X or $7.5 million. Remarkable, isn't it?

> **One amazing thing about cash flow streams is that they are valued as a multiple of their annual cash flow.**

The multiple that is applied to a CFS is impacted primarily by its predictability, expected duration, and future growth of the CFS. Higher predictability or confidence in the future cash flow, expectations of the sustainability of the CFS, and the future growth rate all increase the multiple of the cash flow. This *multiple of cash flow valuation* concept is just a shortcut to the present value of future dollars calculation we discussed in Chapter 4. The same is true for commercial real estate and the CFS of its rent or the price of the stocks of companies with great earnings and dividends.

Even though such knowledge defines how wealth creators think, it's not commonly discussed with employees or students studying to be veterinarians.

Bottomline: to become a prosperous veterinarian, we must acquire assets that produce CFS that grow every year and are valued as a multiple of their annual payments. The main paths for us include: practice ownership, real estate, and dividend paying stock investing. These are patterns you must recognize. Sure, there are others, but these are the high probability, proven, and well-traveled paths.

Remember, as a licensed veterinarian, you have a regulated and protected right to the CFS of a veterinary practice! A closer examination of these three paths will produce an understanding that can be easily transferred to other situations.

Path #1: Practice Ownership

JW "Finally, have a seat at the table."

That's the case I make to a veterinarian considering practice ownership for the first time. When you are an associate veterinarian, you are the economic driver of the business, but you have no *say* in it. Most of us want to have a say. For example, if you think it's to the benefit of the clinic to donate time to a spay-neuter charity, and you start going up the corporate chain of command to get that approved, it usually doesn't happen. You work hard. You have the best interest of the practice at heart. You know the community. And yet nobody listens to you. Instead, you take direction from someone outside of your community who rarely listens to you.

Time and again, I've heard a story similar to this: you get a mandate from the regional manager who parachutes in for a half-day once a quarter and says, "We're going to change the staffing model to X, Y, and Z." Meanwhile, you're thinking, "Are you kidding? That's going to create all sorts of friction in my day if we do that." You may lose your best technician whom you've trained from day one, who now knows your every move and can complete your sentences. But now she's virtually gone for the sake of a new "staffing model." And that's just one example of how little say non-owner vets have.

But what if you had a seat at the table?

What if the decisions within the four walls of your hospital were yours to control? Such control can allow for a lot of happiness to follow. It's said the difference between expectations and reality is where happiness lives—imagine managing both sides!

> **What if the decisions within the four walls of your hospital were yours to control?**

The veterinary practices of today operate in three fundamental business models: Independent, Corporate, and Hybrid.

The Independent Model

AA These are legacy practices, typically owned by one or two local veterinarians. They are fiercely independent and value the control they have over their lives and the activities within the practice. Let's call these the *"Independents."*

The Independents are declining in number due to the corporate consolidation of our profession. Many owners of Independent practices have been the beneficiaries of this trend, having sold their practices to consolidators for many millions of dollars. They have taken this wealth and created financial freedom. The high value of the practices has eliminated the historical path to practice ownership for young veterinarians. The Independents woke up to find their asset was worth too much to sell to their young associates with no capital.

The future of Independents remains excellent. Afterall, independent practices are a great asset. They produce reliable cash flow streams and are very resilient to economic cycles as a result of how highly we and our clients value our pets. If an independent practice is in a good location and has multiple veterinarians, it will continue to be sought after by larger veterinary service organizations (VSOs) and may be sold when the owner is ready to monetize their practice asset.

Remember that predictability of cash flow—and the minimum reliance on the owner or any one veterinarian to generate the revenue and the growth rate of the practice's cash flow—greatly influence the valuation multiple of its CFS. Single practices are always less valuable than groups of practices or platforms because their CFS are at greater risk. "All your eggs in one basket" goes a long way to summing up this fact.

If you are an owner of an Independent practice, being smart about investing your excess cash flow to build other unrelated CFS in dividend paying equities and real estate is key to your future success.

The Corporate Model

The second business model active in veterinary practice today is the pure corporate model. These are the organizations like Banfield, NVA, VCA, BluePearl, Southern Veterinary Partners, Thrive and so many others. This model is the reason so many of us have become employees and not owners. Occasionally, these businesses offer some equity-like incentives but fall short of giving veterinarians a true seat at the table.

Let me assure you, these organizations are not *evil*. They serve a different set of masters than the Independents and Hybrids (discussed ahead). They are complex, system driven, and designed to compound their owner's capital. Their owners are usually institutional investors who are working to create financial returns for their partners who may be teacher's pension funds, state employee retirement funds, large foundations, or wealthy families.

Corporate organizations have their share of positives: quality of care measures, training program investments, and career pathing, among others. They're also strong on introducing a brand concept to the profession and providing an exit route to so many Independents. There can be a sense of safety and stability that comes with the corporate world, particularly in terms of benefits, salary increases, and job security. In contrast, entrepreneurship can seem riskier and more daunting, especially for those with family responsibilities or who feel unsure about where to begin.

At its best, the corporate setting offers a supportive approach to leadership development, mentorship, and association. Rather than pushing individuals to climb the corporate ladder, the focus is on personal fulfillment and leveraging strengths while addressing weaknesses.

At the same time, the corporate model is uniquely positioned to benefit from your dysfunctional relationship to money and prosperity. They are happy for you to be an employee and to contribute to the compounding of their capital. Out of necessity, they must centralize control and bring in "managers" to help them protect and grow their investment. This centralization of decision-making by non-veterinarians is at the core of our dissatisfaction with the corporate model. We air our frustration in terms of "failed culture" and our organization lacking soul.

> **The corporate model is uniquely positioned to benefit from your dysfunctional relationship to money and prosperity. They are happy for you to be an employee and to contribute to the compounding of their capital.**

Know this—the veterinary schools are listening to these corporations. Perhaps consciously or not, schools are filling their classes with people who are more likely to become employees than owners. This, however, is a source of great opportunity for you. Regardless of what the AVMA espouses, we are living with a shortage of veterinarians. (Remember, in today's world it really takes two vets to equal one vet of twenty years ago because of our part-time attitudes.) Corporations are spending millions every year trying to recruit a finite number of vets. Inherent in this shortage is the opportunity for you to set a new course—to take control of your life, transform our profession, and be happier.

The Hybrid Model

The third and final business model is the Hybrid model. The Hybrids are a fusion of the best of the Independent and Corporate models — where the contributions of the organization's business acumen are combined with the veterinarian's clinical, entrepreneurial, and leadership skills — and each are rewarded.

For over twenty years, Chip has built new veterinary practices with talented, entrepreneurial veterinarians as partners in their own practice. Following the sale of our practices, I was asked to consider involvement in CityVet by its financial sponsor. I saw the Hybrid-model as the perfect opportunity to bring my talents to bear, helping veterinarians take back their economics, become more prosperous, and transform our profession.

The Hybrid model is the great reawakening of veterinary entrepreneurship. Given capital and business support, veterinarians can co-develop and build *cash flow streams* in practices they co-own. This is effectively moving a great deal of wealth onto veterinarian-owned balance sheets. This occurs, of course, because the ultimate source of the practice's CFS is the client and their selection of a practice and veterinarian to perform services for their pets. The Hybrid model is where the rubber meets the road for your unique engine of prosperity.

> **The Hybrid model is the great reawakening of veterinary entrepreneurship.**

Hybrids are built on the belief that veterinary practices are best run by veterinarians who are owners and can make the most important decisions closest to patients and veterinary teams.

CityVet's approach to leading is to practice *servant leadership*. Servant leadership means identifying the needs of the people you lead and meeting them. Notice it is *not* meeting their wants! Servant leaders are "others focused," not self-focused. They carry the trait of humility. They will always do the right thing for their people and their organization. In some cases, these may not be reconcilable, and so the health of the organization must be satisfied so the needs of more people can be met. I've always loved the expression, *"bad for the hive, bad for the bee."* Our interdependence on each other is often underappreciated. A servant leader must balance these tensions to gain influence and lead from a principled stance.

Hybrid models are uplifting in the sense that the markers of a healthy culture abound. Low turnover, fast decision-making, patient-focused systems, and healthy growth are all common in these practices. While nothing is perfect, and these practices face many of the same challenges any practice faces regarding staffing, recruiting, training, upset clients, grooming mishaps, and more, the difference is the decision-*maker* is right there, working in real-time to solve problems and move forward with kindness and support.

> ### RISK *AND* REWARD?
>
> **JW** Most young aspiring veterinarians either see themselves in white lab coats with a stethoscope around their neck or jumping out of their well-equipped truck at a farm to care for animals. The possibility of practice ownership seems a given. It's not until we gain some real experience in the field that we discover practice ownership today comes with big challenges—the start-up costs, the responsibility, the financial risks, and the uncertainty about retirement, among others. The question is—*is the risk worth the reward?*
>
> For me, early on, I didn't make the connection between practice ownership and cash flow streams. My approach to finances centered on living within my means, avoiding excessive debt, and making basic investments without taking unnecessary risks. I didn't have a formal education

in personal finance, and while I did attempt to gain knowledge by trying to read books like *The 10 Day MBA* (I made it to day 6), I didn't delve deeply into financial strategy or small business ownership. I did, however, have an entrepreneurial bug constantly buzzing in my ear.

My perspective began to shift from risk to reward during my time running an ophthalmology consulting business in a variety of clinical settings including "condo style" in multi-specialty facilities. While I didn't shoulder all the responsibilities of hospital ownership, I was exposed to different models of business ownership and I started to recognize the control and economic result it offered.

When I transitioned into a more corporate environment, I learned more about size, scale, efficiencies, and leverage. While profit distributions in corporate settings aren't typically making it back into the hands of individual practitioners, there can be significant investment in large scale programs, benefits, and growth, bringing long term stability. A great option and one that doesn't limit a person's ability to learn to invest, buy real estate, or develop a product.

In the corporate setting of BluePearl, I didn't associate my entrepreneurial bug with any pursuit in the veterinary world. Instead, I felt I needed a creative outlet and something that I had more control over. So, with my partner at the time, we ended up starting an ice cream company. Learning about an entirely different industry, experimenting with all the yummy flavors, and ending up with a neighborhood shop was really hard work and really fun. We wanted the product itself to end up in freezers across the country, but I ended up sticking with veterinary medicine and he stuck with his original career.

I remember talking to one of the founders of BluePearl when he was curious about what exactly I was doing with this whole ice cream thing—*was I really considering leaving vet med in hopes of becoming an ice cream mogul?* I explained that I just needed to feel more ownership and control in my life. I couldn't quite see it in my veterinary career.

Ice cream wasn't going to be the path for me, but it was important to truly understand what Andy means when he refers to passive income and cash flow streams (CFS).

Most veterinarians are like me. We focus on maintaining a comfortable lifestyle and making responsible financial decisions without fully grasping the potential for building a cash flow stream. While some may save for their children's education or seek advice from financial advisors, there is generally a lack of understanding about optimizing practice income and leveraging it for future growth.

My focus now, through Arista Advanced Pet Care, is on helping veterinary specialists and emergency doctors build CFS as owners in their own practice. Now that I know what I know about cash flow streams, I can't "unsee" it, and we get immense joy from helping other veterinarians achieve it. We're helping veterinarians transform the art of their practice into lucrative cash flow streams and prosperity. When practice ownership evolves into a sustainable CFS, individuals often experience a profound shift in their happiness and stress levels.

A noteworthy story coming out of CityVet involves one of the original partner owners. She opened her own practice and then expanded to multiple locations. She enjoyed the journey, benefited from it personally and financially, and recently made the transition to a leadership role within the home office team as vice president of clinical development now focused on helping others follow in her footsteps.

We have many stories of veterinarians who discovered a new opportunity beyond their clinical practice. While some choose to remain practitioners indefinitely, others may feel drawn to explore different paths or pursue leadership roles within the industry.

If you're considering practice ownership, here's the best piece of advice I can offer: don't be afraid of diving into the financial side. Becoming financially savvy doesn't detract from your dedication to your profession or your compassion for pets and pet owners. There are ample opportunities to give back and make a positive impact, even as you focus on financial security.

Many people feel overwhelmed by technical details, but mindset matters more than mastering every aspect of financial intricacies. Adopting the right perspective is key to success. As veterinarians, we are natural learners who thrive on new challenges. It's not too much of a stretch for us to embrace the mindset that managing finances can be rewarding rather than daunting.

By shifting our perspective, we find that understanding financial concepts becomes more manageable and fulfilling. We don't have to become an expert overnight—even a basic understanding can yield significant benefits in the long run.

Building a cash flow stream requires patience, learning, and a willingness to confront fears and uncertainties head-on. By gradually building confidence and understanding, we can empower ourselves to make informed financial decisions that align with our goals and aspirations. Because, yes—the reward is worth the risk.

Path #2: Investing

The first rule of making money work for you is paying yourself before anyone else. By "pay yourself" I mean save for your investing activities before you pay any bills or have any fun. The targeted savings rate should be 15 percent of income—but starting with 10 percent when you are young is fine, too.

Assuming that by now you've completed the financial course we recommended and have built a budget, paying yourself should be the first line item on it. This discipline will set aside the funds to start your investing activities and fuel your compounding toward prosperity. If you learn nothing else from our work, I hope you will take this and put it into practice. Paying yourself first also helps those of you (like me) who are inclined to overspend.

Investing is like cruciate repair techniques before the development of Tibial Plateau Leveling Osteotomy. There were so many techniques described you could be certain there wasn't a clear winner. By the same token, there are so many books on investing and thousands of people earn their living selling and implementing the many investment approaches. I think it's safe to assume no one approach is perfect, and there is no one-size-fits-all approach, because things like age, risk tolerance, income needs, and other factors come into play.

For veterinarians, I almost always recommend an independent financial advisor (not a broker or "insurance guy") because of our limited understanding of money and investing. Most of us are sitting ducks for the unscrupulous or bad actors of the financial world.

After you have completed a personal finance course, you will be positioned to understand the basics and work intelligently with a financial planner. I like the "Certified Financial Planner or "CFP" certification as a reliable screening tool for selecting someone with whom to work. Remember that if they are selling any products or charging a commission, run the other way until you become an expert and can assess the risks of the investments. Certified Financial Planners, meanwhile, work as a fiduciary for a known fee. They should help you assess different asset classes and where to access them.

Working with a CFP and a Registered Investment Advisor who is a fiduciary is a great combination. Make sure the advisor is also paid based on your success. They should earn better fees as your assets grow. Lastly, make sure you find and affiliate with a CPA and a business attorney. You need both for their wise counsel as you build your financial independence. Get plenty of references and interview several before making a selection.

I like the stock market for several reasons: it compounds, is relatively stable, and is convenient to access at a low cost. Once you begin the flow of savings into an account, it can then be invested in accordance with the plan you and your advisor develop. By the way, if you are employed and have access to any retirement accounts that have employer matching programs, invest there to the extent the dollars are matched. That said, if you intend to invest your savings in things like a practice or real estate, you may not want to over commit to these types of accounts because, while they have tax advantages, your money is trapped there until retirement (unless you pay a big penalty).

Generally speaking, I like to see people invest in stocks that have paid and grown their dividends for decades along with low-cost index funds that track the broad US stock market. Dividend-paying stocks provide a CFS that you receive quarterly. You can use these returns to meet living expenses or to reinvest in more stock.

> **I like to see people invest in stocks that have paid and grown their dividends for decades along with low-cost index funds that track the broad US stock market.**

The best stocks also continue to grow their earnings and stock price over time. As they grow their earnings, they continue to grow their dividend payments as well. If you reinvest your dividends (don't spend them) you are participating in compounding.

In the pages ahead, we introduce you to Will Verity's firm, VIP, which has committed its entire business strategy to managing portfolios for clients to produce cash flow streams and grow the value of their accounts. Later in life, when they have reduced their need to work, the clients use the cash flow stream(s) to pay for living expenses and normally allow the principal to continue to grow in value. As of August 2024, Verity manages over $125 million of veterinarian-owned assets that generate over $4.0 million a year of passive income. (Full disclosure, I am a client of Will's firm, serve on his board and investment committee, and have a small ownership position.)

The place to start investing is a self-managed brokerage account at Charles Schwab, Vanguard, or Fidelity. As your savings accumulate, they can be invested in a low-cost Exchange Traded Fund (ETF) or a mutual fund in dividend-paying stocks. Expect that these investments will fluctuate enough to make you uncomfortable at times. Your main advantage is time. Make sure you do not fall victim to your emotions but rather follow your advisor's advice to stay the course.

The fact that your investment in a stock gets re-priced every second the markets are open is challenging. It's nerve racking and it leads many investors to move in and out of the market at the wrong time as a result of loss-aversion bias. If you are not familiar with the field of Behavioral Economics, please approach Nobel winners Kahneman and Tversky's work on the subject, which shows how people don't always act rationally as traditional economic theory suggests and links our behavior as investors to social influences, cognitive biases, and emotional responses. (Kahneman takes these concepts further in a later work, *Thinking Fast and Slow*, which delves into how our brain uses two distinct processing systems to make decisions.)

Investing in this way builds a reliable store of compounding capital that can be easily paired with practice ownership and our third category of wealth creation, real estate. For younger, would-be veterinarian owners, I think of a dividend paying stock portfolio as the "waiting place" for capital. It is there, working and compounding, but is available if a higher-returning opportunity presents itself, like investing in a practice or a great real estate opportunity.

> **For younger, would-be veterinarian owners, I think of a dividend paying stock portfolio as the "waiting place" for capital.**

While "retirement" drives much of the investing conversation for most, I believe we should reject the old paradigm of "retirement." That's because our view of work must evolve beyond a single career to include all the activities we integrate to help meet our total wealth objectives.

Everyone has the need to pay their later life expenses without working as hard as they have been for most of their careers. No one wants to be a burden to their children or society. But thinking about investing solely in terms of later-life funding is overly limited. In fact, it is a dangerous bet.

Nowadays we are often living to 90-plus years of age. If you still use 65 as a retirement age, this means we must:

- Spend 25-30 years to grow up and acquire skills;
- Work 30-35 years to produce wealth;
- Survive on the funds from our working years for another 20-30 years.

I like to think of this in terms of a 30/30/30 formula. The second 30-plus year period must not only fund its *own* expenses but produce enough savings and investment to contribute meaningfully to funding the last 30-year period and, if possible, leave something to the next generation. If that won't get you motivated, I don't know what will.

To show you what I mean, we've broken out a simple progression of *Financial Wealth Levels* in Figure 1. These are a general guide to the progression we normally see in veterinarians, business owners and other healthcare providers. (In Chapter 6, Chip aligns these five levels with the five stages of a veterinarian's development.)

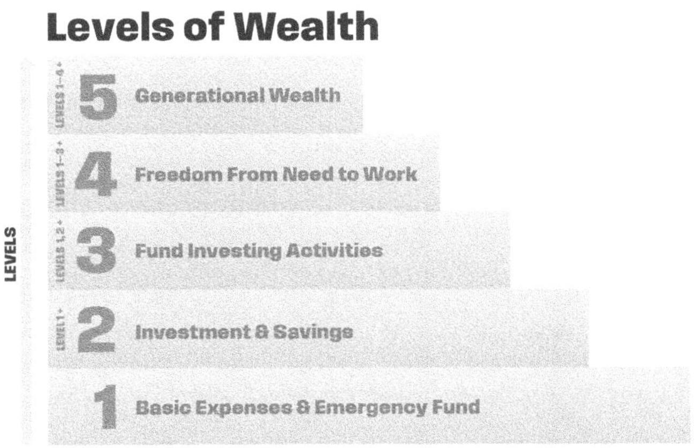

Levels of Wealth

5 Generational Wealth (LEVELS 1-4+)

4 Freedom From Need to Work (LEVELS 1-3+)

3 Fund Investing Activities (LEVELS 1,2+)

2 Investment & Savings (LEVEL 1+)

1 Basic Expenses & Emergency Fund

LEVELS

Figure 1: Financial Wealth Levels

"GETTING THE LINES TO CROSS"

Will Verity is a longtime friend (35 years and counting!) and business partner. Will founded Verity Investment Partners twenty-five years ago with the goal of helping others build sustainable passive income that produces financial freedom.

When Will talks about financial freedom, he calls it "getting the lines to cross," a phenomenon which typically occurs between Levels 3 and 4. This is when you have all the basics covered, are enjoying your investments in cash flow streams, and are starting to experience freedom from the need to work.

But we don't start here. All of us start at the bottom, earning income the same way. A veterinarian's income can come from three primary sources:

- work as a professional (trading hours for dollars)

- ownership of a practice that produces cash flow
- investments in assets that produce *cash flow streams* (passive income).

To go from Level 1 to Level 2, the total of our after-tax income must be greater than our expenses by enough to meet unforeseen or emergent needs and to save for investing activities.

Going up the Levels means building wealth by replacing income from work with predictable passive income. If we are good savers and investors, the passive income we build from our assets will eventually allow us to decrease the amount of income needed from work ("work deceleration") to cover expenses (including debt repayment), savings, and emergency funds.

When passive income alone is sufficient to cover our needs, **The Lines Cross**. The following graph depicts how this concept works.

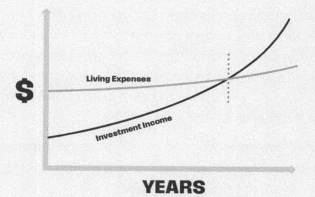

Figure 2: Getting the Lines to Cross

Getting the lines to cross may not be possible (or even desirable) for everyone. A life rule espoused by Will's Grandfather was, "If you rest, you rust." I tell veterinarians describing a retirement of total leisure to "do this at your own peril." I think of many people, including my father, who declined rapidly in the old retirement paradigm. Many died prematurely of chronic illness brought on by the effects of a *Purpose Deficiency*. We need work of some sort—or at least a strong Purpose—to be healthy.

Path #3: Real Estate Investments

CC For any veterinarian dreaming of owning their own practice, the *building* and the *business* are often intertwined. "Wanting to hang your own shingle" implies the two are one and the same. Today, while many aspiring practice owners see owning the property as an integral part of their dream, it's harder to achieve now than it was in the past. Even so, we believe it's an endeavor well worth the pursuit.

You are more equipped for real estate success than you realize. Here's what I mean: When you start a practice, you develop skills in evaluating your location, demographics, rental options, and more for your new business. Despite this learning experience, few veterinarians translate these skills into real estate investing. We get exposed to the basics of market analysis and real estate fundamentals, and we go no further. That's a missed opportunity.

> **We get exposed to the basics of market analysis and real estate fundamentals, and we go no further. That's a missed opportunity.**

Beyond the allure of owning property, commercial real estate offers a distinct set of advantages and opportunities that every investor should consider. For many investors, including myself, the intrinsic value of property and the Cash Flow Stream that real estate provides just feels different from all other investments; it feels more solid, more tangible, more *real*.

Our goal is to lay out the basic elements and benefits of investing in commercial real estate and illustrate its significance as a strategy for wealth creation and portfolio diversification.

In my early days as a veterinarian, I started investing in commercial real estate by securing a purchase option as part of the first practice lease I signed. As soon as the practice was producing a healthy CFS, it became an asset I could borrow against. I used the practice's CFS to fund the purchase of the real estate by exercising my purchase option. I now had a second healthy CFS. Hence the importance of developing your pattern recognition skills.

After getting my first taste, I realized the impact it made on my balance sheet, so I went back for more. I repeated the process with my second practice and its real estate, and then did it again a third time, and again each time that option was available.

I quickly learned to love real estate for its distinct financial advantages. Foremost is the ability to *leverage* ("use borrowed money") the purchase of real estate, which enabled me to secure my first property with a minimal down payment and use the cash flow of my practice to pay off the debt. My *equity value* in the property came from both the *appreciation* of the property and the *rent revenue* generated by my practice as the tenant. These attributes made it an attractive investment for me, much like dividend-paying stocks.

Soon, I discovered the tax advantages, which truly made me fall in love with real estate. Real estate allows you to deduct the interest payments from the rental income, reducing taxable income. Another tax advantage is the *depreciation* of buildings and improvements, which further reduces taxable income but does not use cash flow. Additionally, when commercial real estate is sold, we can reinvest profits into other properties, deferring the capital gain taxes owed through tax sheltering programs unique to income-producing property.

Interestingly, our unique position as veterinary practice owners allow us the opportunity to be an attractive borrower for both the business and the property. And since veterinarians have a reputation for ethical operations and low default rates, we earn top marks for creditworthiness.

The big takeaway is that veterinarians are well-suited to be good real estate investors. We already possess the foundational skills one needs to approach real estate investing. And while terms like "net operating income" and "leverage" might initially intimidate us, we soon realize we're often already applying these concepts.

We also tend to be conservative by nature, striving to negotiate the best deals possible, which begins with a fair purchase price, and sets us up for success. Plus, real estate's long-term investment horizon aligns well with our patient and disciplined approach. It's a natural fit for us, given our commitment to making things work and our willingness to invest in the future.

The bottom-line: Investing in commercial real estate offers a compelling compounding opportunity to produce passive cash flow streams, diversify investment portfolios, and build prosperity.

A REAL ESTATE PORTFOLIO

There's no need to stop at owning your practice's location. There are many different types of real estate, and advantages that come with each. Personally, I've diversified my investments into real estate through various avenues, including REITs (Real Estate Investment Trusts), limited partnerships, and syndicated deals in commercial real estate. Commercial real estate may seem intimidating at first, but really it shares similarities with owning your practice or your home.

Let's break down a typical scenario: suppose there's a Starbucks property in Columbus, Ohio, selling at a price where the rents are five percent of the purchase price. This means that if you paid all cash, you'd receive a 5%

return. However, leveraging the investment, typically with a 15% to 20% down payment, changes the equation. Yes, interest rates might currently surpass the 5% return, but if you can tolerate the initial shortfall, future rate reductions could yield significantly improved returns. Factoring in real estate appreciation and tax benefits, the net return could reach the low teens, a concept often overlooked by investors.

Leveraging (using debt) essentially involves making a purchase with a fraction of the total cost paid in equity. For instance, with a million-dollar property purchase, a 20% down payment reduces the initial outlay to $200,000 while using $800,000 in debt or "leverage." Similar principles apply to purchasing single-family residential properties.

Commercial real estate presents distinct advantages in lease structures. Unlike single-family homes where landlords often bear tax and maintenance responsibilities, commercial tenants typically cover these costs, simplifying the return calculation. Overall, commercial properties offer a more lucrative investment opportunity when compared to residential properties.

Starting with nothing except grit and determination, I took it upon myself to meet hundreds of real estate professionals and experts and learn as much as I could.

Today, I'm at the point where dozens of emails flood my inbox daily advertising for various commercial investment opportunities. Once you start, chances are you won't stop, and the cash flow stream opportunities become limitless!

At the end of the day, cash flow streams — whether from medical practices, dividend-paying stocks, or real estate — are key to supporting your ability to be prosperous.

SUCCESS OUTSIDE THE CITY

We will close with the story of Dr. Forrest and his wife Rachel, who built their lives and practice in a small town in South Carolina. The population of their trade area had started at around 10,000 residents and grew to 15,000 over their career. They had a terrific practice and ultimately opened a second location. They recently harvested their investment through a sale of the practices to a corporate buyer. Forrest has continued to be involved in the practice. His honest take on working in a practice without owning it is this: "It's very different when you don't own it—you just can't fake the commitment."

Rachel played a key role in building their financial freedom. She served as practice manager and financial officer for the business. She also expressed her creativity through their real estate investing. Rachel was the main driver of remodeling Airbnb homes they invested in as rental real estate. Her goal was to make them a "cool" place for those visiting their area. From Rachel's background in pharmaceutical sales, she learned the practical aspects of how "business" was conducted, which proved invaluable in co-building the veterinary practices with Forrest.

Forrest's father had been a veterinarian working in pharma. When Forrest discovered his interest in the life sciences, his father encouraged him to be a dentist for a sure path to a great income. Forrest took the MCAT and considered human medical school after being accepted, but ultimately he followed his heart to veterinary school. Just before beginning vet school, his father sent him a newspaper clip stating that there would be a glut of veterinarians for the next ten years along with a note telling him he could still change his mind. Undeterred, Forrest said he knew he and Rachel could "figure it out."

They deployed all the strategies we have discussed. They owned and sold their practices for several million dollars. They invested their excess earnings and capital in dividend paying stocks and rental real estate. Today they have complete financial freedom and are pursuing their passions. Forrest is an accomplished artist and Rachel continues to design and execute value-building projects in their real estate portfolio.

They have even undertaken to refurbish (while living there) a famous home on the water built in 1855 appropriately called "The Oaks," which served as "Hospital #1" in the Civil War. There is some discussion of the presence of ghosts of fallen soldiers still inhabiting the home. I'm unsure, but standing in their magical home you do feel the presence of a different time and the weight of our country's past.

I love Forrest's and Rachel's story for several reasons. First, I admire their complete partnership in life. Second, I love seeing a veterinarian succeed and achieve comprehensive prosperity. And third, I like that they're doing it all in a smaller community. Life in a small community means, "you're not anonymous," as Forrest says. People are more accountable, and you feel you can make a greater impact on your community. Forrest and Rachel have a deep faith in their people and are thankful to have been able to build a great life of service in a wonderful place.

CHAPTER 6

THE FIVE STAGES OF THE FINANCIALLY PROSPEROUS VETERINARIAN

By Chip Cannon

I'm a veterinarian, practicing since 1995. I'm also an active investor, primarily in commercial real estate. And I'm the founder of CityVet, which has grown from a single practice location to a nationwide organization that promotes veterinarian owned and led clinics. We believe that veterinary care is best delivered in a practice materially owned by an onsite veterinary partner who is also a servant leader.

From the beginning of my career as a veterinarian, I knew that I was always on the path to building *prosperity*, but not because my priority was to be "wealthy" in a financial sense. Always wanting to make more than just money, I'm thankful that from an early age, in my most formative years, I was pointed to something higher than material success. The concept of **Comprehensive Prosperity** captures it all.

My walk of faith has guided me to pursue my *calling* at each stage of life. Ingrained in me is the belief that our ultimate pursuits should be focused on being who God made us to be and doing what He made us to do. And when we make our *callings* our highest priority, we are on the right path to living our highest Purpose and afforded the best chance to achieve a life of freedom and prosperity.

For most of us, professional freedom includes practicing the way you want to and caring for your patients and clients the way you feel called to. For some, freedom means transitioning from full-time employee to full-time *parent* and part-time veterinarian. For others it means having ownership in a practice you lead, building a team, and managing a culture aligned with your own values. And at some point in life, it also means having the freedom to choose when you work or even if you work as a veterinarian at all.

For me, even before I went to vet school, I had a calling to own my own practice. Why? Freedom. Freedom for myself as a practitioner, and the complete freedom to take care of my patients, clients, and team the way I felt called to. Then, from owning one practice to having two, from two to four, from four to ten and so on, I had a calling, to grow and scale our business. Why? Freedom. A calling to create more freedom for me, and more freedom and prosperity for others, too.

Our success with CityVet has certainly blessed me with the freedom to pursue my highest Purpose as a husband and father, and to serve our business and my community. Now my highest Purpose is growing our model of co-ownership at

CityVet to help provide more opportunity to as many veterinarians as possible, especially those who are at the point in their careers where they are ready to own their own practice and lead their own teams. Helping provide these opportunities to other veterinarians, who may not be able to or want to do it on their own, is the part of my work and prosperity that I am most thankful for.

After a thirty-year career striving to build comprehensive prosperity for myself and others, I've reached a point where I now realize that the financial aspects of prosperity come in steps and stages. Understanding these stages is critically important to achieving them.

In my experience, there are five general stages to becoming a financially prosperous veterinarian:

- **Stage 1:** *Acquiring Skills* – becoming a competent and confident practitioner
- **Stage 2:** *Proficiency and Productivity* - becoming a proficient and productive practitioner
- **Stage 3:** *Divergence* –realigning priorities of life and career
- **Stage 4:** *Building Assets* – becoming an owner or investor or both
- **Stage 5:** *Harvesting Assets* – enjoying maximum freedom (financial and non-financial)

Stage One: Acquiring Skills

I didn't start at the top. In fact, when it comes to financial prosperity, like most veterinarians, I started at the *bottom*.

Rewinding the clock thirty years, my starting point was like many in our profession. We all enter the veterinary field driven by a desire to care for animals, a trait deeply ingrained in us as nurturers. Initially, the priority for most of us is to become competent and confident practitioners.

I chose my first job as a veterinarian based primarily on the opportunity that would give me the best chance to acquire skills—i.e., the job that would give me the most varied experiences and provide the most support and guidance to quickly become a competent and confident practitioner. Of course, I needed enough compensation to pay my bills, a schedule that wouldn't kill me, and a location that my wife and I could tolerate. But building wealth at that point of my career was all about becoming a good veterinarian *first*.

In stage one, most veterinarians are satisfied if their income from their first salary is sufficient to cover their basic expenses with a little left over for a favorite hobby and a nice vacation. This stage matches up with Level 1 Wealth from Chapter 5, where basic expenses are covered by your income, with sufficient surplus to establish an emergency fund. Ideally, though, you approach stage one as the beginning of intentional wealth-building habits, like paying yourself first. Here, with very specific intention, you should begin learning about basic financial principles that include budgeting, stewardship, controlling expenses, saving, giving, and investing.

> **Approach stage one as the beginning of intentional wealth-building habits, like paying yourself first.**

Stage Two: Proficiency and Productivity

After my first job working in mixed practice, taking emergency calls more nights than not, I was ready for the next stage. My priorities shifted from fast-tracking skill acquisition to wanting a different work environment where I would have the freedom to practice higher quality medicine, have less emergency call, and enjoy the opportunity to earn more money and start saving. This is a very common description of the shifting priorities typical of the second stage of most veterinarians' careers. After you gain some competence and confidence, the thinking evolves from 'can I do the job,' to 'how can I do it *best*' and 'what *more* can this job provide for me?'

With some experience under my belt and the confidence to become an earner, I moved to my home town, Carrollton, Texas, for a better opportunity. There I joined the practice I had worked for from my early teens through college. It was a modern practice owned by a veterinarian whom I admired as a good leader and practitioner. I learned a lot from him, but more from observation and association than from formal mentorship.

I grew as a practitioner for sure, but the greater learning I received from him was in how to take care of people. He was (and still is) a good man, and to see how he cared for clients in his special way had a real impact on me. I could also tell he genuinely cared for his staff, which included me. He blessed me with the opportunity to work hard and take on as many cases as I could handle, which helped me grow in my proficiency as a practitioner and enjoy higher compensation with a less demanding schedule. In stage two, I was experiencing productivity and the fruits of it.

The path to prosperity at this stage of my career was focused on maximizing the opportunities available to me as an employed veterinarian (a better practice, culture, leader, schedule, etc.) and the fruits of hard work (more freedom, financial and non-financial). I enjoyed this job and this stage of life with its new freedoms for a couple of years, but I was already sensing the urge to take my next step.

Most veterinarians at this point are evaluating their compensation more critically, as they should be. Am I being compensated fairly for the work I am doing and the revenue I am producing? Should I be making more, could I be making more? Could I make more and work less? Or could I work more and make more? These are appropriate and important questions to evaluate.

Ideally, this stage of wealth building (the beginning of Level 2 Wealth in Chapter 5) is focused on learning to optimize earning potential so as to maximize funds available for both life activities (family expenses and fun) *and* investing. In stage two, we must actively start to invest meaningfully. Putting a few dollars into a company sponsored retirement plan is good, but that approach is not enough to build prosperity. This is the stage where we as veterinarians tend to fall behind on the path.

> **We as veterinarians tend to fall behind on the path.**

Stage Three: Divergence

After veterinarians have experienced productivity and the professional growth their first one or two jobs can provide, the paths for veterinarians often start to diverge.

Divergence is the stage where you re-evaluate your life priorities and current work situation to determine if they are aligned with what matters most to you. If you decide they are not, the result leads you to make changes that can have a big impact on wealth-building and happiness. Unbeknownst to those who have not been intentional about learning financial concepts in the prior two stages, these decisions can greatly impact your path to financial prosperity and freedom. As Andy pointed out, make sure your financial health is a part of your analysis, as "every decision is a money decision."

Divergence is the stage where you re-evaluate your life priorities and current work situation to determine if they are aligned with what matters most to you.

Typical shifts in this stage include:

- Going from full-time to part-time, because the priority has become more time to parent, play, rest, or simply work less.
- A shift from employment to self-employment such as relief work, for those who want more control of their schedule. (The opposite shift, for those doing relief work and wanting to get back to enjoying the benefits and stability of employment, may also occur.)
- Going back to school or onto specialization.
- Seeking career advancement in management, leadership, or other opportunities in the profession or outside of it.
- A calling to pursue practice ownership and the various paths to prosperity it provides.

The opportunity in the divergence stage comes from evaluating whether our non-financial priorities are greater than our financial priorities. *Are my financial priorities aligned with my current financial trajectory?* Whether or not the non-financial priorities rank above or below the financial ones, if the financial priorities remain focused on simply covering one's personal expenses, investing (for financial freedom) continues to take the lower priority.

Look at it this way: investing should always be given appropriate consideration and prioritization in full light of one's ultimate goals. Some practical examples of investing decisions a veterinarian may face during the divergence stage include:

- *If I make a change to work less, how will it impact my ability to invest and my future financial goals?*
- *How will switching from employment to relief (or vice-versa) impact my investing goals, expenses, and chances for financial freedom?*
- *If I take this new job to make more current income, should I spend the extra income on a newer car, bigger house, or should I invest more or pay off debt faster?*

Financial planning and investing must be equal parts of a comprehensive evaluation when considering a change in one's path. Because no matter the path chosen, investing significantly impacts wealth in all its forms. And here is the kicker—the ability to take healthy steps towards the last two stages of wealth-building depends on the choices you make at this third and critical stage of *Divergence*. Here in this stage, debt should become secondary (or no longer a factor), while your savings and investing should develop significantly as you make meaningful contributions to your strategies.

Stage Four: Building Assets

Veterinarians by nature seem to adopt an admirably conservative and more frugal approach toward spending money. The trouble is, this same conservative approach is often applied to the pursuit of prosperity, which may result in underinvestment in understanding financial concepts and in building assets.

Most of us are aware of the basic tenets of personal finance: you need to make more than you spend, save and invest what you can, and prepare for retirement. But we usually overlook or lack understanding of what's really required for prosperity.

Typically, our asset-building efforts are rudimentary at best. We work to retire debts, buy a home and a car, contribute to our 401(k), and then invest in mutual funds. We fail to learn the power of investing earlier, investing more, and exploring the options for investing that could yield higher returns. It's all too common for veterinarians to reach mid-career before they start paying attention to investing and the power of asset building.

As a result, many veterinarians find themselves stuck in a cycle of working to cover expenses and funding their current lifestyle without any progress toward financial freedom. Most evolve from living paycheck-to-paycheck to living a very comfortable life while working. But by stage four, you should be watching your portfolio of assets grow in a predictable way and considering new ways to obtain the benefit of passive cash flow streams. You should be experiencing the compounding effects of your early investments.

> **By stage four, you should be watching your portfolio of assets grow in a predictable way and considering new ways to obtain the benefit of passive cash flow streams.**

Assets appreciate and depreciate in value. There are assets that produce income and those that do not. As we have discussed, to achieve financial freedom, one needs to own assets that produce cash flow streams (CFS). Assets that only grow in value but produce no spendable cash flow may produce good returns. Certain types of stocks, land, and bitcoin fall into this category. Note that these will have to be sold, the taxes paid, and the proceeds converted to assets that produce cash flow at some point to become a CFS that supports your life.

Planning around the sale of assets is the typical retirement strategy. Savers often pursue investing with the hope that they end up with enough assets to sell in retirement and live off the proceeds. While this may be a viable "retirement plan" for some, it isn't a viable plan for building wealth and financial freedom to enjoy before retirement.

Building prosperity and freedom for the short-term *and* long term requires building assets that produce growing passive income *today*. Some asset classes do that, but many do not. Let's look at some examples:

Non-Cash-Flowing Assets:

- Cash under the mattress
- Cryptocurrency
- Depreciating automobiles and boats
- Jewelry, art, and gold
- Non-dividend paying securities (mutual funds and stocks)
- Retirement accounts not invested in dividend-paying companies
- Land
- Homes

Cash-Flowing Assets:

- Business ownership with profit distributions
- Commercial real estate that produces rent
- Dividend paying securities (i.e., certain classes of stocks)
- Private debt that produces interest
- Residential rental property
- Royalties
- Bonds, money market funds, and savings accounts

The key question is: Are you building a portfolio of assets that produce growing CFS?

To unpack that, ask yourself:

- Are you spending all you make or are you dedicated to minimizing expenses so there is always money left over to invest in wealth-building assets?
- Are you investing in assets that appreciate or depreciate?
- Are you investing in cash-flowing assets or non-cash-flowing assets?
- Are you leveraging your degree, your skills, your efforts, and your leadership potential to build assets like owning a practice or inventing a medical device?
- Are you using the assets you currently have (home equity, cash, stocks) to leverage investment into other assets like real estate?
- Are you pursuing greater knowledge of financial concepts and investing, as part of your growing core competencies?

Regardless of the path you choose or the steps you take to build assets that produce CFS, the goal is to reach the fifth and final stage of becoming a financially prosperous veterinarian, which is characterized by the freedom to enjoy your life fully on your own terms.

Stage Five: Harvesting Assets

In the financial world, harvesting an asset traditionally means selling an investment to realize its appreciation (or loss). But I believe harvesting can also mean enjoying the returns of an investment's cash flow *without* having to sell it until you are ready. Selling assets that have been owned for at least one year also produces a lower tax rate called "capital gains" when compared to ordinary income. Capital gains treatment may reduce your tax rate by up to 50 percent or more. This tax treatment highly incentivizes investors to hold assets and time such harvests to achieve the lowest possible tax treatment.

> **Harvesting can also mean enjoying the returns of an investment's cash flow *without* having to sell it until you are ready.**

The ultimate freedom is to have enough assets producing cash flow streams that enable you to choose whether you keep an asset and continue to enjoy its current income or sell it if you think it has reached its peak value. Being in this position is a characteristic of Level 4 and 5 wealth-building. Your money is working for you, and you get to choose the timing of your harvest.

For veterinarians, the harvest stage could look something like this:

- You have ownership in a veterinary practice that is producing healthy earnings;
- You have added dividend-producing stocks and/or real estate investments that together produce cash flows sufficient to cover all your needs (which means you could stop working as a veterinarian if you wanted to).

More typically, most veterinary practice owners still need the money they earn from working as a veterinarian to support their desired lifestyle and savings because they have not built other cash-flowing assets outside of their practice. In these situations, Level 4 and 5 wealth can't be achieved unless they were to monetize the value of their ownership by *selling* their practice. Historically, this has been the most common storyline for veterinarians that have owned their own practices.

Fortunately, for those who own multi-doctor practices with healthy profits, the past decade or more has been a good time to harvest the asset value of their practices. Their challenge has been determining if the sale proceeds are large enough to purchase other cash flowing assets sufficient to maintain their desired lifestyle in perpetuity—or would they need to spend the principal to cover expenses? Such an extremely important cash flow analysis should be supported by a skilled financial planner or analyst, as the answer may significantly change the timing or minimum valuation of an owner's sale transaction.

For those veterinarians that have owned single or two doctor practices without strong cash flow, the outcome has most likely been different. These practices, as assets, are valued much lower than their larger peers, because their cash flow streams are small and are at a high risk of eroding once the long-term owner is no longer practicing. These owners are working longer and seeking creative ways to fund the last part of their lives. At the same time, these smaller practices may serve as buying opportunities for younger veterinarians. The new owner might relocate the practice or otherwise overcome the prior owner's growth limiting conditions. Growing a single doctor practice to a mulit-doctor practice is a great strategy for creating prosperity.

For those veterinarians contemplating the right moves to get to this final stage of financial prosperity, and ultimately to harvesting assets, the consideration of practice ownership is an incredibly important one. You want your life's work of building a practice to have the best chance of becoming a valuable asset, one that is appreciating every year and producing CFS for you and creating multiples of the CFS in asset value for future harvest. In the next chapter, we'll examine how to build and harvest assets through practice ownership.

For veterinarians, it *might* be possible to reach Level 4 and 5 Wealth and its freedoms *without* having ownership in a practice if one starts investing early, wisely, and aggressively (as Brent showed us in Chapter 4). But for the average veterinarian like me, without family money or a winning lotto ticket, practice ownership should be the first consideration for building assets to harvest now and in the future. Comparing the returns on investments available to me over the past three decades, there has been no better performing asset than the investment I made in myself and my partner veterinarians through our practice ownership.

CHAPTER 7

BUILDING CASH FLOW THROUGH THE HYBRID OWNERSHIP MODEL

By Chip Cannon

If and when you reach the point in your career where you can own equity in a practice either as a partner or solo owner, a pivotal shift occurs. Instead of creating value for someone else, you're now creating equity value for *yourself*—an important step toward comprehensive prosperity.

Wise Choices Matter

When starting your own practice, making wise choices from the beginning is critically important, especially considering the challenges facing independent veterinary owners today. With more deep-pocketed corporate competition than ever before, there continues to be a growing commoditization of many veterinary services and products into alternative delivery channels, along with a shortage of veterinarians and support staff to build quality teams. It seems more challenging than ever for the independent veterinarian to be able to compete. These and other factors make it even more critical for those starting new practices to make wise decisions from the beginning.

The list of critical decisions to make when starting a new practice is long. A full discussion is beyond the scope of this book, but a short summary includes choosing:

- The right market demographics, psychographics, competitive landscape and demand metrics to support a multi-doctor, multi-million-dollar practice.
- The right physical location with high visibility, accessibility, and appropriate zoning, entitlements, etc.
- The right facility size—not too small and not too big.
- The right lease terms.
- The right floor plan, design, mechanical, electrical plumbing, equipment, etc.
- The right marketing plan, technology plan, and human capital plan.
- The right budget and source of capital.
- The right leadership plan.
- The right business systems.
- The right business support team and ops plan.
- The right strategic plan.
- The right team, the right culture—not to mention the execution of it all.

Making wise choices from the beginning sets the course for the type of asset the practice will become. And the sobering truth is that you need to get all of these critical decisions right (or mostly right) in order to have the chance to build a high-performing asset. Any one of these decisions can impair the value of the practice.

The main point here is that even though practice ownership is the best path for a veterinarian to build wealth, it isn't an easy path, and it's harder today than ever before. The risks are significant and require careful analysis, comprehensive planning, expert advice, consistent execution, and ongoing support. The rewards are worth the effort for those that do it right.

A Different Approach: Co-Ownership

As for doing it right, there is a different approach with new options for veterinarians considering practice ownership today. A Hybrid or co-ownership model, the model we developed at CityVet, is a veterinarian-centric ownership model where you can partner with an experienced practice developer and operator to co-create and co-own the practice together. At CityVet, for example, we have twenty-five years of experience developing successful practices and have become really good at making those critical decisions for opening a practice and then providing industry-leading business and leadership support to our partner veterinarians. This enables our veterinarian partners to worry less about the risks, while still enjoying all of the rewards of practice ownership.

CityVet, as of this publication, supports over fifty practices in eight states. Each practice is significantly owned by a local veterinarian (most around 40 percent) who receives compensation as a clinician, leader, and owner on a monthly basis. Such partners have taken a giant step forward in creating their own powerful *CFS*.

CityVet and Arista (the specialty and emergency brand), meanwhile, provide the capital, real estate services, technology, marketing, financial consulting, accounting, and mentorship to its veterinarian partners. Over 70 percent of CityVet partners are women. None of them had any business experience before becoming a partner, and almost none had any material capital to invest.

One of the additional benefits of our model is that our veterinary partners may have periodic opportunities to monetize portions of their ownership. They get to harvest the earnings of their asset every month in the form of profit distributions, and they may have the potential to harvest the value of their equity, in part or in whole, opportunistically.

In other words, the practice as a CFS provides partners with options. They can consider re-investing the cash flow into another practice or in alternative investments. Their cash flow and equity can provide the basis for additional borrowing capacity as well. We've had veterinary partners invest in multiple practices and experience remarkable financial growth and freedom as a result.

That's why we believe so strongly in the prosperity-building power of the co-ownership option. It provides more veterinarians with the opportunity to realize the dream of practice ownership. And it provides the freedoms only ownership can provide—the freedom to *enjoy* being a leader, an owner, and a veterinarian—without having to carry all of the risks and burdens on your own. What really sets CityVet apart is that we empower veterinarians by igniting their entrepreneurial spirit at the stage in their career (Divergence) where they are ready to be owners and leaders. We give them the freedom and coaching to become the leader only they can be.

Practice ownership is not for everyone, but don't short-change yourself by assuming it isn't even *possible* for you. Our industry desperately needs more veterinarians in the driver's seat of practices. Veterinarians acting as servant leaders of veterinary teams who care for clients, pets, and each other is what our industry really needs to be transformed. Don't get derailed by the assumption ownership isn't possible —maybe it is!

IT STARTS WITH DESIRE AND COURAGE

Andy, Jennifer, and I often observe a reluctance among veterinarians to take advanced steps toward asset-building of any kind. Sure, many go beyond basic budgeting to setting goals for increasing discretionary income and savings. Yet they often stop short of deploying income in ways that could compound and grow their *prosperity*. And while some may invest, it's without thorough planning, particularly regarding cash flow and estate planning.

I knew nothing at the beginning of my journey—I started only with the desire to gain freedom. But as I've worked my way through the stages, I've come to understand the

> importance of continuous learning and proactive asset growth, and it has all been fueled by the desire to learn and the courage to act.
>
> It's never too late to start. By paying attention, staying mindful, and actively seeking to understand how to grow one's asset portfolio, veterinarians can progress through the five stages of wealth and build comprehensive prosperity.

A Story of Building

In the past, if you were an associate without a practice to buy and you had the courage and confidence to start your own, you would typically find a growing suburb on the outskirts of a metropolitan area, where new houses were being built. There, you would establish your practice, often leasing a small space and hoping to expand over time, eventually hoping to own your own building.

In my case, after trying and failing to buy the practice in my hometown, I wanted to take a different approach to starting my own practice. I wanted to skip the initial step of leasing a small space because I knew it would limit future growth.

I studied successful multi-doctor, multimillion-dollar practices and identified the factors contributing to their success, including real estate selection, demographics, and facility size. I wanted to build a practice that could accommodate multiple veterinarians from the beginning, but I lacked the funds.

Typically, a veterinarian needs about 0.3 to 0.5 acres of land to build a practice, but land parcels are often sold by the acre or more, making desirable parcels unaffordable. Some veterinarians make the mistake of buying too much land and building too large, strapping themselves to high occupancy costs, while others build too small, limiting their ability to scale and build a healthy cash flow stream.

To overcome these challenges, I approached a developer with a proposal. I explained that I needed a smaller parcel of land but couldn't afford it unless it was purchased as a larger parcel and divided. I offered to assist with the grunt work to find potential tenants for a retail center the developer could build on the remaining parcel. In exchange, the developer agreed to carve out a portion of the land for me to build on.

Together, we put the deal together in Flower Mound, Texas, securing the land under contract. We spent several months and many dollars putting the plans together, doing the legal work and submitting for preliminary city approvals. But just days before we were to finalize the contract, an undisclosed easement problem killed the deal.

I was heartbroken. More than a year of effort had been invested in this endeavor. And here I was with no backup plan, no income, and a brand-new mortgage—my wife and I had just purchased our first home. But in many ways, I was at peace, trusting that God had better plans for me, and that He must have some lessons for me to learn. (I've learned both are always true.)

Just a few weeks later, a friend asked me to join him in attending a Christian men's group meeting in downtown Dallas. Fortunately, I now had extra time on my hands.

The meeting place happened to be situated in the heart of a gritty but thriving urban area of Dallas known as Oak Lawn. I began attending these meetings on Thursday mornings at 7 o'clock, accompanying my friend downtown.

About three weeks into our routine, as I exited the highway onto the road leading to our destination, I encountered a roadblock caused by a fire in a nearby building. Forced to navigate through the back streets, I found myself within two blocks of the fire, surrounded by hundreds of spectators, *each with at least one dog on a leash.* It was a striking sight that captured my attention, prompting me to reflect on the potential opportunities for urban infill practice locations.

This experience became my "burning bush" moment. I delved into research comparing demographic densities between growing suburban developments, urban infill areas, and the transitional spaces in between. I also studied the psychographics to understand how different levels of discretionary income and spending habits were influenced by demographics.

For most veterinarians seeking a new practice location, urban infill locations like this were typically avoided due to the parking challenges and difficulty obtaining zoning permits for pet-related uses. But I saw a lot of potential in the area.

In suburban areas, families with children and pets may have higher discretionary incomes, but they tend to allocate less of their budget to pet care due to other financial obligations.

But in densely-populated urban areas, where pet ownership rates are high and many residents are young professionals or empty nesters, spending on pet care is often greater. These individuals prioritize their pets' well-being and are willing to invest in their care.

Back to the "burning bush"—recognizing the untapped potential, I approached the landlord of the burned-out building and proposed a partnership to renovate the space. I would lease the damaged space and accept the challenge of renovating it if, in exchange, he gave me an option to purchase the property at the end of the first term of the lease. To my delight, the landlord agreed, marking the beginning of CityVet.

Before signing the lease, I was also compelled to approach the three nearest veterinarians. I contacted each, asking for the opportunity to stop in and speak with them. Meeting each in person, I expressed my desire to get their blessing to put in my new clinic as I wanted to start on good terms, preferring to be their colleague rather than their competition. This approach was disarming, and I even became friends with all three. Interestingly, the closest one eventually became my first acquisition once he decided to sell his practice.

Acquiring that second practice made me realize that the quickest and most effective way to cultivate a culture of care, i.e., the key to our success, is to have an owner *present* who truly cares, all day, every day. This owner can best demonstrate to every client and, more importantly, to their team, how to provide exceptional care and delight clients, and how to take care of each other as teammates, especially in tough times.

This, in turn, fosters the culture of care, which is crucial for success. The owner's level of care and kindness sets the tone. There is no better person for this role than a veterinarian who truly cares about pets and *people*. This realization laid the foundation for our CityVet hybrid model.

I partnered with two veterinarians, Dr. Erin Tate and Dr. Matt Murphy, for the second practice, which we promptly turned around from struggling to success, mirroring our first practice's performance. From then on, I continued this pattern, reinvesting every penny I earned, navigating through the challenges of bootstrapping growth.

By the time I started the second practice, private equity and corporate practices had roared onto the scene, making veterinary owners uncomfortable in many ways. As independents, we all feared losing our advantage because corporations could scale in ways we couldn't match—buying power, marketing, HR benefits, and so forth. I saw how our Hybrid Model could level the playing field.

> **I saw how our Hybrid Model could level the playing field.**

It became clear to me that to stay relevant in today's and tomorrow's marketplace, veterinarians needed to focus on what I believe matters most, what we excel at, and who only we can be: *caring veterinarians in leadership positions, as owners!*

Owner veterinarians make the best real-time, on-the-ground decisions, not only to care for patients and clients but also to support their teams in ways that corporate practices can't. This realization became a *new calling* for me—to put veterinarians back into ownership and provide today's and tomorrow's veterinarians with opportunities we were losing.

The challenges are much harder now. Back when I was searching for my first practice, corporate practices weren't a significant factor because they weren't starting new practices (apart from Banfield). Today, corporate entities and private equity groups are starting new practices, too, leveraging their vast resources to secure prime locations, putting even more competitive pressure on the independent veterinarians. This has also led to the creation of several new de novo models (new practice models). Since the new de novo models are owned by non-veterinary owners (private equity, corporations), their strategies may have the same weaknesses as the consolidation approach.

Our approach stands out because, as veterinarians, we make colleagues our co-owners. We have a solid financial history spanning more than twenty-five years—a track record that few others can claim. As of this writing in 2024, we have 50-plus co-owning veterinarian partners, with 25 more in the pipeline for next year. Each of our partners are building prosperity and financial freedom on their own terms, as true practice owners.

A Closing Word on Prosperity and Freedom

Prosperity, in my view, is synonymous with freedom. It encompasses personal, professional, financial, and cultural freedoms that enable us to pursue our highest calling and make choices aligned with our highest Purpose. True prosperity is the unrestrained ability to live a daily life of peace, joy, and fulfillment, where we love what we do and those we do it with.

While financial abundance is part of prosperity, it should not be the ultimate goal. True prosperity lies in the freedom to build, lead, and sustain a culture of care and love within our families, workplaces, and communities. This pursuit involves caring for others and creating the conditions that allow us to continue doing so each day, thereby enriching our lives and the lives of those around us.

To me, this means that the pinnacle of true prosperity comes from spiritual and emotional prosperity, not material wealth. It involves recognizing that true freedom cannot be attained by prioritizing success, material possessions, or even ourselves, above loving others. Spiritual maturity is reflected in our willingness to love and serve others in every aspect of life, even when it costs us something, and the result that comes is the spiritual wealth of peace, joy and fulfillment.

Put another way, you aren't ever "rich" if your balance sheet is healthy but your heart is empty.

CHAPTER 8

ON ENTREPRENEURSHIP, MENTORSHIP, AND ASSOCIATION

By Chip Cannon and Jennifer Welser

CC Years ago, I provided some guidance to a struggling partner, Dr. M, who was dealing with staff retention issues. At the time, we had an established formal review process and best practices for staff engagement. But during my conversation with Dr. M about retention, it became evident that her approach seemed rigid and robotic, solely focused on following the system.

I offered to spend some time at her practice to observe firsthand. What I discovered was that while her team respected her as a skilled veterinarian with a commanding presence, there was a perception that she didn't genuinely *care* about them individually, despite her own feelings. While she said she valued her team, she wasn't demonstrating genuine care and connection with team members in ways they could feel and trust. Sometimes we forget the value of human interaction and empathy in fostering strong relationships within the workplace.

So, we sat down, and I offered her some advice. I said, "Let me tell you what I did with my very first practice. When I hired my first staff of five, I asked them to make two promises."

The first: "I'd love for you to join my team. But I need you to promise that no matter what's going on in your life or how your day is going, or how you roll out of bed, when you get here, you promise me that you'll commit to joining me and your teammates in doing everything you can, giving your best effort to delight every client that walks in the door—promise one."

Promise two: "do the same thing for your coworkers. Delight each and every one of them with your care."

Now, she had heard those two promises. But then I said, "Now, as a partner, I want you to promise that you will come in, day in and day out, and be intentional about showing each and every one of your team members that you truly care. Delight them as their leader."

That's all I had to say. Just be intentional. Show them that you care. Show them that they matter—and find ways to do it each and every day. And so we brainstormed. We said, "Okay, that might be, 'Hey, so-and-so, how are you doing today? I know it's a busy day. Is there anything I can help you with?' Or 'How can I make it better for you today?' Or a simple 'Great job' or a pat on the back or a high five?"

Dr. M started practicing the techniques and the change was immediate, because it was real. She became mindful about showing her team members that she truly cared and demonstrating it in ways she hadn't before. And it made all the difference for her and her team.

I share this story because it exemplifies the most important thing we can do as an *entrepreneur*, which is to build and maintain a healthy culture of care. A culture that everyone benefits from.

> **the most important thing we can do as an *entrepreneur*, which is to build and maintain a healthy culture of care.**

Entrepreneurship

When it comes to my understanding of "entrepreneurship" as a veterinarian, I've always felt a bit uncomfortable with the term. On paper I may be an entrepreneur, but I haven't always identified as one—for me, I think of it as just following a calling that has evolved over time.

Initially, we enter this profession driven solely by a desire to help animals. As time goes on, our aspirations and paths diverge, shaped by individual experiences and goals. I've observed many veterinarians who never considered entrepreneurial efforts until reaching a point in their careers where they felt they had mastered their craft and sought new challenges. It's at this juncture that they begin contemplating possibilities they never thought attainable before.

But what about the term "entrepreneur?" Why is it so hard for us to identify with it? Perhaps it's because when we think of the word, we're more likely to think it describes someone like a Silicon Valley tech company founder. Or perhaps because it doesn't fully capture the type of "entrepreneur" we want to embody.

Looking up the word in the dictionary, we see its French origin describes someone seizing an opportunity and building upon it. But to me, a true entrepreneur isn't solely driven by personal gain but also by *a desire to help others benefit as you do*.

Recently, in talking with a friend, I discovered the term "redemptive entrepreneur," which encapsulates the kind of entrepreneur I strive to be. Even in the beginning, when I had no business training or experience, I started with the desire to build an organization that would profoundly impact pets and people.

A redemptive entrepreneur isn't solely focused on personal gain; instead, they aim to help others along the way. Their profitability isn't just about their own bottom line, but serves as a test of value and viability for everyone involved. They see their work as a means of improving the lives of every customer, pet, and team member they encounter. They prioritize making everything better for everyone they touch—or, as I like to say, reconciling "Heaven to Earth" through their work. (In my view, following divine principles in business yields divine results. We can make good profits that *bless everyone involved*.)

> **Profitability isn't just about their own bottom line, but serves as a test of value and viability for everyone involved.**

Sadly, there are too few businesses that prioritize the well-being of all stakeholders, focusing instead on profit margins or the interests of a select few. Many entrepreneurs fall into the trap of being exploitative, solely focused on personal gain with little regard for others. Or some may run ethical businesses but lack the mindset of prioritizing the betterment of *everyone* involved. Such business philosophies are the most common, unfortunately, but they come with hidden costs and often these costs are paid by the workers. While these models may yield short-term temporal gains, they don't produce long-term rewards.

A redemptive entrepreneur seeks success for everyone involved, not just owners and investors, but also the employees, customers, partners, vendors, and greater community. Love for others should be everywhere in business. Remember, "Work is Love made visible." That being said, many people limit this love to their personal lives, prioritizing their families but neglecting to extend it to the people in their work. This is a missed opportunity.

Redemptive entrepreneurship (and a redemptive business) requires us to infuse every aspect of our work with love for people. When we approach our work with this mindset, the results (financial and non-financial) surpass those of any other business model.

STEWARDSHIP

For me, it helps to adopt a *stewardship* mentality rather than an ownership mentality, even when we are the owners. Recognizing that nothing truly belongs to us, the redemptive entrepreneur sees work as a gift to do good with—good for everyone. Stewardship, therefore, challenges the instinct to solely prioritize revenue and profits, especially at the cost of something or someone else.

Behind every decision, virtue should be the driving force. Our ambitions must align with the highest purposes of doing good for all, prioritizing this mission over profits alone or exit strategies.

A virtue-driven approach means always doing what is right and doing the best possible for your clients, team, community, and investors combined. It means paying staff the most that can be afforded rather than the least they will accept. It means going the extra mile for customers to show them you truly care and practicing "unreasonable hospitality" (please read Will Guidara's book, *Unreasonable Hospitality*). From supporting vendors and not squeezing them, to giving back in the community; it's all about producing *good* profits, not just profits. Good profits are the profits earned when *everyone* involved in the work and transaction is blessed by them.

> The virtue-driven, redemptive approach for business is vital for fostering the healthiest cultures of care that truly edify teams, consistently delight customers, and withstands all challenges.

Mentorship and Association

When I began my career thirty years ago, there wasn't a standardized expectation to receive mentorship as part of your first job. Young professionals were valued for their ability to learn independently. Many of us didn't have the luxury of extensive mentorship opportunities. My first job was helping an overworked veterinarian stretched too thin who had little time to guide me, forcing me to learn on the fly primarily on my own. This was a common experience for many in my generation.

But times have changed. New graduates today face different types of pressure, including a more litigious society, instilling a fear of legal repercussions if outcomes aren't perfect. Consequently, mentorship has become an essential benefit for the new graduate, and for avoiding potential trouble. It's disheartening to see this shift, but it reflects the reality of our current world.

Still, I grapple with the idea of formalized mentorship. While there is a need for structure, I believe fostering a culture of servanthood should be inherent in our efforts. Every individual, not just leaders, should be eager to support and guide their colleagues, regardless of their tenure. Mentorship shouldn't be viewed as an extra effort but rather as a fundamental aspect of our professional community.

Every workplace should foster a culture of mentorship and a genuine desire among colleagues to help each other thrive.

> **Every workplace should foster a culture of mentorship and a genuine desire among colleagues to help each other thrive.**

In my own journey, associations have played a pivotal role. And when I say "association," I am referring to the people that I sought out to lean on and learn from, who were willing and kind enough to help me. These were the informal mentors I could pick up the phone and call or go have a cup of coffee with. These were also my formal advisors, like my accountants, attorneys, and bankers. Active participation and intentional networking with experienced individuals have been invaluable to my learning and growth. Without these connections, I wouldn't have reached the level of success I enjoy today.

Associations can also be both formal and informal groups of professionals who share knowledge and experience in some group setting. These can be formal associations that meet at conferences or local business groups that have regularly scheduled get-togethers (like Young Entrepreneurs Organization), or even—most informally—just a few folks at a coffee shop or on a Zoom (like one of the investment groups I am in).

Let me emphasize one point though: Many young professionals today approach associations passively, akin to how interactions unfold in high school, where you connect with whomever happens to be around you. That being said, the best associations are formed proactively. It's about identifying individuals and organizations that take the initiative to support your growth and development. For veterinarians who want to be owners and/or investors, this means seeking out individuals, specialty groups, and experienced advisors who are willing to share their knowledge, wisdom, and expertise.

As an entrepreneur, I recognize that there is always more to learn, especially in areas outside of my formal education. Practically, that means I must seek knowledge firsthand from a variety of non-veterinarians.

For example, learning the basics of business, such as accounting, marketing, HR, financing, and legal matters are crucial skills needed to enhance one's professional journey. We didn't get much on that in vet school, and even though I spent a lot of time studying these topics on my own, my most valuable and efficient resources to further my business education were my associations.

Another important point about associations is that they should include those at different stages of development in relation to you. You can associate with peers, who are at a similar level in your field, sharing experiences and exchanging skills, benefiting each other mutually. You can also learn from those who aren't in your field but who share similar challenges (like other small business owners or real estate professionals).

There is always value in being the least experienced person in the room.

You often learn the most from those with more experience (and intellect) than you. Learning from these mentors is invaluable for personal growth. If you lack this level of association, your learning journey will likely stagnate.

Associations, by definition, are your relational capital—they are the people you trust to share ideas and problems with, those who have the right motivation to help you learn and shape your plans. For entrepreneurs, active engagement in associations is crucial—you can't become a great steward or truly redemptive entrepreneur based only on what *you* know.

At CityVet, we've intentionally built a partnership model that embodies this concept of perpetual mentorship and association through true servant leadership. Our model provides the highest and most holistic association of professionals in veterinary medicine and in the business world, fostering a culture of personal development. We strive to equip young entrepreneurs with everything they need to excel not only as veterinarians but also as leaders, managers, and business owners. From legal and accounting to marketing and HR, we provide access to expertise and guidance, empowering our partners with all they need to make informed, wise decisions. We are all aligned for the growth and benefit of everyone on our team, with our first priority being our partners in the way we support them and their personal growth.

Entrepreneurship

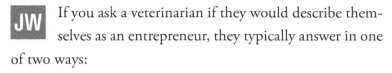 If you ask a veterinarian if they would describe themselves as an entrepreneur, they typically answer in one of two ways:

- "Oh no, I'm not nearly visionary enough;" or,
- "No way, I could never endure the risk of failure."

Veterinarians who start their own practice aren't necessarily aspiring entrepreneurs aiming to change the world or even implement a set of business efficiencies and do things by the book from an MBA standpoint. Most come from the perspective that they would like to (finally) have control over their day-to-day life—how clients and staff are treated; how they build the practice of their dreams. Seeing a practice as a cash flow machine is not typically the initial motivation. Instead, we gradually start to recognize, as a business owner, that we have more opportunities to shape and influence our practice according to our vision.

In the early days of building our New York practice, there was a passionate veterinarian who led the ER department. When we were growing, he had a powerful and positive influence on the culture. With time, as the corporation grew, he became less happy in his role as a "leader," not because he was bad at it, but because in the corporate setting, he was becoming more of a manager and enforcer rather than a visionary and a builder. He found outlets and continued to be a champion for the profession, and he had a young family to support so a guaranteed income wasn't so bad! But he was no longer in the right place.

Eventually, he left and bought a struggling practice. At first just one. With his leadership and the space to make it his own, growth happened. Fast forward to today and he, David Bessler, is the owner of VEG, the largest group of veterinary emergency practices in the country. He leads his business with many of the same core values he struggled to employ back in the corporate setting. By all marks he's a great leader and entrepreneur, and he's found his place.

While many of you may not readily identify as leaders or entrepreneurs, you might identify with the frustrations of your current work environment:

- No control over pricing, staffing, your schedule, or your service quality
- No voice to effect change and positively impact culture
- Feeling trapped by a non-compete or lack of a safety net to make a move
- No passive income

Like Dr. Bessler was, perhaps you're the right leader and entrepreneur, but just in the wrong place!

Entrepreneurship for veterinarians is most typically associated with practice ownership. There are those who have always felt a desire to own their own practice and those who never considered it until they gained more experience and began noticing all of the options out there. Regardless, the prospect of ownership can be daunting. You can write a business plan, go to the bank and/or friends and family to secure funding, and then start in! You can do it solo or with partners. You can also consider a hybrid approach like we offer at CityVet and Arista.

I was recently asked why I didn't just go start my own large multispecialty hospital—*I have the knowledge after all, right?* Wrong. What I do know is that such an endeavor is very hard. I don't want to pretend for a minute that I am an IT expert or that I know how to market or that I know how to negotiate leases and contracts. And I *know* that I don't want to spend a Sunday afternoon figuring out payroll and taxes.

I wanted the best of both worlds—the autonomy, ownership, and prosperity-building of independent ownership, plus all of the support and functional expertise from a corporate size and structure. I want the pendulum swinging in our profession so that we can provide more models and opportunities for all veterinarians to thrive and grow throughout their career.

INVENTORSHIP

Another subset of entrepreneurship is *inventorship*. Part of being a good veterinarian is being a clever problem-solver. You might not realize how some of the problems you solve can lead to products and innovations that are not only worth sharing, but could create an income stream. For product development, my story isn't one leading to early retirement—but I have had a lot of fun and learned a lot along the way.

When I was early in my career practicing, I would recommend oral lysine for cats suffering from chronic recurrent herpes virus. It wasn't until I personally had a cat that needed it that I realized how impossible it was to actually give it to your cat. Giant tablets or capsules for humans crushed into cat food was the only option. So I decided to figure out how to make it easier. I bought a kitchen scale from Williams-Sonoma (which I have to this day) and ordered raw lysine powder from a chemical company to see how soluble it was. I ended up filing a patent for oral gel format lysine in dial-a-dose packaging and then I started looking for a partner to license the product to.

The patenting and partnering aspects were so foreign to me, but my partner at the time was a business guy, and what seemed challenging to me was what he viewed as the easy part. The product launched as Enisyl through Vetoquinol. I enjoyed royalties for a period of time but in the end, I abandoned the patent process, the company "dissolved" the licensing deal, and I was cut out after making enough money for a down payment on a condo and learning a lot of lessons. (No regrets!)

My next product was inspired by watching clients struggle to give their pets eye medications. It isn't easy and the reasons why vary, but I developed UnoDose, which is a now-patented single use applicator for drops and ointments. With the help of two partners, there are prototypes and we have had a couple of licensing deals that seemed promising, but currently we aren't doing anything to bring it to market. I'll pick it back up someday because I believe in the product and the problem it helps solve.

There are plenty of examples of veterinarians developing products, and while the goal isn't to make a penny off any and everything, you should have a basic understanding of intellectual property and the pursuits of sharing your solutions! With entrepreneurship and inventorship, the sky's the limit.

Mentorship and Association

When it comes to mentorship in our field of veterinary medicine, it starts even before we are in veterinary school. Most of us had mentors who played a role in getting us to school. Then, once in school, our professors became mentors to us during our training.

Initially, we expect to learn the black and white facts of medicine, only to discover that veterinary practice is the fun and challenging gray art of science. Rarely is there one right answer. More often, asking three people about treating a disease yields five different answers. This realization underscores the importance of mentorship and the value of modeling yourself after practitioners whose approach resonates with you, both clinically and in terms of communication style.

As you progress, you can see the applicability of mentorship beyond clinical practice. You realize you can seek guidance on your career choices, running a practice, identifying business opportunities, and developing leadership skills. Mentors can provide valuable insights and help you grow.

Mentors are also key to helping you build a network. Generally speaking, veterinarians are introverts and not naturally inclined to networking. Women can be particularly reluctant to network or even ask for help. While I'm not introverted, I was very slow to realize the power of mentorship and networking—*I wouldn't want to burden someone or expect any favors!* It turns out, networking is about learning and sharing, and veterinarians are very good at those!

> **Networking is about learning and sharing, and veterinarians are very good at those!**

Ultimately, mentorship (and growing a network) is a mutually rewarding pursuit. Mentors find fulfillment in guiding others, and mentees benefit from their wisdom and experience. Connecting people with others feels good and sends the message that you care. It really is that simple, and you never know where conversations and relationships will go.

I strongly encourage you to seek mentorship, networking, and involvement in communities both within and beyond the veterinary industry. Don't confine yourself. If you don't know where to start, pay more attention to all of the networking opportunities scheduled at literally every conference you've ever attended—and go to them! Call an old classmate. Send a message to a professor you are grateful for. Talk in depth to a neighbor with a different profession.

When I was practicing as a veterinary ophthalmologist, deeply immersed in my ophthalmology world, it never occurred to me to attend any meetings that weren't ophthalmology-specific. When I became the Chief Medical Officer at BluePearl, I realized I had been missing out on so much within my profession. Beyond veterinary-focused events, look in your community for groups such as small business entrepreneurs' meetings and networking events. Any community group or event you are involved with is an opportunity to network with people. Be a joiner and don't let those opportunities pass you by.

I was very fortunate during the phase of my career in Mars Veterinary Health to have access to large and diverse non-veterinary networks and executive coaches who taught me so much. I don't take for granted how valuable those experiences have been. Not everyone has the opportunity to join *Women 50*, a high-level networking group, but the most valuable lesson was that the opportunities for growth are everywhere when you start looking. I discovered the value of discussing challenges, seeking advice, and learning from inspiring people outside the veterinary realm.

For example, when discussing a challenge with individuals *inside* your industry, you may spend too much time in the rabbit hole of details, losing sight of the core of the problem. But in speaking with "outsiders," you learn to be articulate and succinct, sharing only what is really relevant. Challenges are often more universal than you would think. Outsiders can offer fresh perspectives, untangled from the minutiae, which can lead to enlightening "aha" moments.

Take the time you spend with others as precious. I tend to be very comfortable in off-the-cuff conversations, but I often get more out of conversations when I've taken the time in advance to think through and even write down what exactly it is I want to talk about or hope to get out of a conversation. You wouldn't walk into an exam room without having read the record and reflected, for just a minute, on what you will say and what questions you will ask. Treat conversations with mentors, mentees, and new connections in your network the same way. Investing time in these endeavors is rewarding and invaluable for personal and professional growth.

On the path to becoming a prosperous veterinarian, we must recognize the value of networking and seeking mentorship, both for our professional development and personal growth. We are entrepreneurs supporting other entrepreneurs. Our emphasis on mentorship is crucial. We acknowledge that veterinarians may find themselves navigating unfamiliar territory without formal education or clear aptitude. By working alongside peers who have either been through similar experiences or are just beginning, there's a sense of camaraderie and shared learning that is highly appealing.

CHAPTER 9
PRACTICAL TRUTHS FOR LIFE

By Andy Anderson

It's going to take something different from you to achieve what you currently lack. In other words, when we shift to building *prosperity and being happier*, a big part of that shift is in our perspective and the tactics we choose to *live by*. In this chapter, we cover the wisdom, mindset, and practical truths that have helped many veterinarians and others on their journey.

So many books of this nature tell you all about *what* to do but offer little in terms of *how* to accomplish your goals and sustain your efforts to take control of your life. Your pursuits will always need support, but in the early days of your new path, your habits and practices matter a great deal. The following is meant to be a helpful but not exhaustive set of principles and actionable steps to set a course toward comprehensive prosperity.

Other than my faith, the three most powerful path-sustaining tools are the ancient philosophy of Stoicism, the commitment to consuming (reading/listening to) uplifting materials that positively influence my behavior, and the utilization of a goal setting and accountability tool (a Life Operating System or LOS, which we cover in Chapter 10). I'd like to spend some time on a few of these practical truths in the hopes that you will connect with them and develop some new and sustainable habits that can be applied in your life.

COMPOUND HABITS

In his book *Atomic Habits*, author James Clear delivers a compelling mechanism for building good habits (or breaking bad ones). He defines atomic habits as "a regular practice or routine that is not only small and easy to do, but also the source of incredible power."

Similar to compound interest, atomic habits provide exponential returns in the long term. An example of improving just 1 percent a day is telling. Imagine if you commit to a new "good" habit with this mindset for one year. Let's say that you can do five sit-ups today and you want to improve just 1 percent a day. You set a target and start at 5 sit-ups. In one month, you are doing 7 sit-ups. In six months, progressing 1 percent a day, you can do 30 sit-ups. In 9 months, you are doing 72 without difficulty. Finally, at the one-year mark you are knocking out 187 sit-ups with no problem and looking for the next challenge. This is a whopping 37X improvement with just doing 1 percent more a day.

This concept is best applied to areas where you have the time for the compounding to work and you are starting from a very low mark. Unfortunately, the concept works in the opposite direction when you deviate from course. The longer you are off course, the greater your miss!

Back in the day when I learned to fly airplanes, we used a navigation aid called a VOR (very high frequency omnidirectional range). They were all over the country and formed highways in the sky that our instruments could detect and follow. If we departed from a VOR on the 090-degree highway (radial) we were flying due east. Let's imagine that we missed our setting by just one degree. After 1 mile of flight, the error was imperceptible—same with 10 miles. But after two hours, we missed our destination completely.

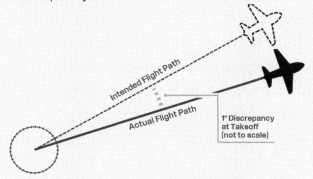

Figure 3: The Fallout of Going Off Course

Getting off track by even a little over a longer period of time is devastating. Habits require frequent monitoring and assessment. That's where an LOS comes in (see: *Chapter 10: A Life Operating System*). It provides a

> cadence so that you check-in frequently enough to not miss the mark. Staying on course with your targets and habits is essential to your outcomes.
>
> Think of the material that follows as your VOR-like instruments for life. These are the things that will keep you on the right course and not allow you to look out the window five or ten years from now and wonder, *what happened?*

Stoicism (Not What You Might Think)

Stoicism, a philosophy developed in ancient Greece and advanced during the Roman Empire is most classically presented by the Emperor Marcus Aurelius in *Meditations*, a collection of his writings to himself in notebooks depicting his version of the Stoic philosophy in terms anyone can live by and practice daily. Practicing any discipline is hard. Marcus Aurelius seems to use his journal as a way to beat the principles into his unconscious mind through repetition.

Stoicism addresses the eternal dichotomy between good and evil in terms of virtue or vice. Virtue is seen as knowledge. The four primary virtuous ideals are Wisdom, Courage, Temperance (moderation), and Justice. As rationality is a fundamental and unique quality of our species, the acquisition of knowledge and its rational application is the bedrock of Stoicism and a Purpose-based life.

Stoicism is a practical philosophy that moves us toward personal freedom, resilience, tranquility, and excellence while preparing us to overcome adversity, uncertainty, and anxiety. We live in an uncertain age. Frankly, we are just like every other time in history. Our threats are different yet similar to those in the past. It is in fact the reason an ancient philosophy remains uniquely relevant today.

Many leaders from different walks of life have used Stoicism to steady their course through challenging times. Some prominent examples include:

- George Washington
- Bill Clinton
- Theodore Roosevelt
- Thomas Jefferson
- General James Mattis
- Admiral James Stockdale
- Cory Booker
- Arnold Schwarzenegger
- Bill Belichick
- Nick Saban
- Ben Roethlisberger
- Tom Brady
- Chandra Crawford
- Michael Lombardi
- John Steinbeck
- Ralph Waldo Emerson
- JK Rowling
- Robert Greene
- Tim Ferriss
- Jack Dorsey

Notably, most of these names are males. Where are the women? In her excellent essay, "Women Don't Need Stoicism; Stoicism Needs Women," Sharon Lebell makes the case that women benefit as much from the Stoic philosophy as men and add the unique superpower of equanimity to the mix. Lebell's book *The Art of Living: The Classical Manual on Virtue, Happiness, and Effectiveness* is a great onramp to Stoic philosophy and its practice, as are various books and podcasts by Ryan Holiday.

Whether you are winning your fifth Super Bowl, leading men into battle, or operating a veterinary practice, such principles matter.

One of the most celebrated principles of Stoicism relates to the application of *Choice* to the process of receiving and reacting to stimulus. (Viktor Frankl expanded our awareness of this concept in his classic depiction of humans under the overwhelming malevolence of a Nazi concentration camp.)[11]

There is a space (or potential space) between our receipt of a stimulus and our reaction to that stimulus. It is in this space that *only* we control, where we can exercise our choice on how to react or feel. This is the space where much of the magic of Stoicism occurs. It is the opportunity to take inputs one might interpret as negative and choose to react with indifference and accept what you are experiencing as the universe's or God's idea of the best path for this moment.

Choosing how to respond to stimulus produces higher contentment. It follows therefore that we can then re-focus on things we can change. The power in this principle remarkably enhances our ability to focus on our pursuits.

Think of all the time you spend reliving the past or anticipating the future. What a waste of energy! Neither past nor future are in your control. You can control only how you choose to respond and the activities that position you for

---

[11] Frankl, Viktor E. 2013. Man's Search for Meaning: The classic tribute to hope from the Holocaust. Random House.

higher probability outcomes. Ignoring what has passed and the unknown future liberates a vast amount of energy and time. Where would you be if you could have all those hours back when you worried about things you couldn't change? Going forward, all that energy and time can become fuel in your tank for pursuing your Purpose and prosperity.

Steven Covey approached this truth with a discussion of two circles.[12] The Circle of Concern and the Circle of Influence. The Circle of Concern is filled by things that we care about but have little or no ability to change. The Circle of Influence is smaller and made up of things we can do something about. The size of this circle is dependent upon one's power and is highly influenced by financial freedom, position, and wealth. Covey points out that those exhibiting his first habit of *The Seven Habits of Highly Effective People*, **PROACTIVITY**, spend their time in the Circle of Influence where they can either directly or indirectly change things. Particularly effective people expand their Circle of Influence to approach the expanse of their Circle of Concern and, in some cases, find their Influence greater than their Concern.

As you begin your journey to take control of your life, remember the lessons of Covey, the Stoics, Frankl, and others that inform how you respond to stimuli and allocate your mental and physical resources in a positive way.

---

12 Covey, Stephen R. 2016. *The 7 Habits of Highly Effective People: The Infographics Edition*. Mango Media Inc.

STOIC PRACTICES

- *Meditate on your mortality.* Memento mori or "remember that you have to die." If you keep this concept close, you will never take yourself too seriously. I use it to ask myself if I am comfortable with a behavior or an investment of time given that I will soon be gone. Is this action consistent with my Purpose?

- *Focus on what you can control.* How much time do we waste worrying about things outside our control by living in the future and in the past? I chose to focus on the intersection of what matters most and what I can control.

- *Live as if you have died and come back.* Imagine the lessons of death. What would they teach you about how to spend your time while alive?

- *Never be overheard complaining—not even to yourself.* Complaining is futile and unattractive. It wastes energy and time for the things that matter most.

- *Tolerance for others, strict with yourself.* You are not here to judge others, but you are in charge of your own conduct.

- *You own everything in trust.* Nothing is yours forever. You are passing through—apply a stewardship attitude in all you do.

- *Put the day, month, and year up for review.*

Put the Year up for Review

I had the idea to extend the Stoic practice of *putting the day up for review* to *putting the year up for review* in an annual letter to my son. Each December, I write about the events of the year, successes, failures, learnings, and yearnings. I think about it like Warren Buffet's annual shareholder letter. Putting the year, the quarter, or the day up for review is part of this Stoic practice.

I like to tell young men and women, "above all else, do not bullshit yourself." Holding yourself accountable and reviewing the period for lessons to carry forward will keep you honest and growing.

> **"Above all else, do not bullshit yourself." Holding yourself accountable and reviewing the period for lessons to carry forward will keep you honest and growing.**

Choose a loved one or small group and write them an annual letter. Compare your targets and results openly and honestly and share what you've learned. Both you and your readers will greatly benefit.

THE STOCKDALE PARADOX

The Stockdale Paradox was presented by my favorite business scholar, Jim Collins, who wrote about it in his must read *Good to Great*. It was derived from an interview he conducted with Admiral Jim Stockdale while walking on the Stanford campus. Stockdale was a prisoner of war and the highest-ranking officer in the Hanoi Hilton during the Vietnam War.

Stockdale attributed his survival as a POW with this mantra: "You must never confuse faith that you will prevail in the end — which you can never afford to lose — with the discipline to confront the most brutal facts of your current reality, whatever they might be." You must hope for the best while preparing for the worst.

At one point on their walk together, Jim Collins asked (excerpt from *Good to Great*):

> "Who didn't make it out?"
>
> "Oh, that's easy," he said. "The optimists."
>
> "The optimists? I don't understand," I said, now completely confused.
>
> "The optimists. Oh, they were the ones who said, 'We're going to be out by Christmas.' And Christmas would come, and Christmas would go. Then they'd say, 'We're going to be out by Easter.' And Easter would come, and Easter would go. And then Thanksgiving, and then it would be Christmas again. And they died of a broken heart."[13]

13 Collins, James Charles. 2001. *Good to Great: Why Some Companies Make the Leap ... and Others Don't*. Random House.

> We don't have to be a POW to apply the Stockdale Paradox to our own life. Whatever painful conditions we're experiencing, we can preserve our hope while at the same time acknowledging reality for what it is. In fact, balancing optimism with realism may be the only functional way of living in this world!

You Are What You Eat

You are what you eat. This age-old truth is applicable to our digestion of information as well as alimentation. Be careful what you choose to read, watch, or listen to, particularly during this time of recalibration and redirection.

There are wonderful books, articles, and podcasts related to the materials we've been discussing. Here are a few to get you started:

- *Meditations*, Marcus Aurelias
- *Love Always*, Bob Goff
- *Screwtape Letters*, C.S. Lewis
- *The Servant*, James C. Hunter
- *12 Rules for Life*, Jordan Peterson
- *The Common Rule*, Justin Earley
- *The Daily Stoic*, Ryan Holiday*
- *Man's Search for Meaning*, Viktor Frankl
- *Build the Life You Want*, Arthur C. Brooks and Oprah Winfrey
- *Falling Upward*, Richard Rohr
- *Tattoos on the Heart*, Greg Boyle

- *The 7 Habits of Highly Effective People*, Stephen Covey
- *Atomic Habits*, James Clear
- *Full-Time: Work and the Meaning of Life*, David L. Banhnsen
- *The Second Mountain*, David Brooks

"*" indicates podcast by same name as well

Freedom vs. Relevance

We often meet entrepreneurs or professionals that are ready to exit their businesses and live the "good life." This is a sure sign of some bumpy times. These lives usually encounter initial infatuation with their ability to relax, play, travel, etc. until they begin to realize that they are not feeling any energy. One more golf game, or trip, or bottle of great wine just doesn't stimulate the same joy as it did a short time ago. You will recognize the role of dopamine here.

An important continuum we encounter in the second half of life is anchored at one end by Freedom and at the other end by Relevance. This is particularly true of those who have developed some level of financial freedom. It is often more of an issue for men than for women because women do not fall easily into the trap of defining themselves by what they do. Rather, many women are better at building community and seeing life as a more balanced equation.

Those who have moved too far toward freedom are often at risk of becoming irrelevant and not of much good to anyone. Such is a symptom of *not* building one's life on solid principles.

With the desire for consumption satiated, the pendulum has swung too far in one direction and they realize they are becoming unhealthy and maybe drinking too much (whether literally or figuratively). The lucky ones self-diagnose and begin their journey back toward relevance (read this as "work") and re-defining their Purpose for this later chapter of life. The unlucky ones begin visiting more doctors and drifting into early dysfunction. We must manage where we stand on this continuum through the techniques outlined in this book. Find your spot and apply intentional effort to your Purpose.

From ancient works like *Meditations* to the recent books by Covey and Brooks, we continue to chronicle truths that help us live more prosperous and happier lives. My experience has been that our education system makes it harder rather than easier to access this wisdom. I've found myself wondering, *how might my path have been different had I encountered these principles sooner?* I'm glad to share them in hopes they offer you some encouragement and new energy for your journey—and none may be more important than the Life Operating System.

> **Those who have moved too far toward freedom are often at risk of becoming irrelevant and not of much good to anyone.**

CHAPTER 10

A LIFE OPERATING SYSTEM
By Andy Anderson

A Life Operating System or "LOS" is a set of practices and relational rhythms that help us create space in our busy world to identify what matters most and do the things to make them realities. An LOS is vital to achieving freedom, happiness and prosperity. I suppose there are many perfectly adequate LOSs. I advocate for this one because of my confidence in its ability to produce results.

Implementing your LOS is a two-step exercise (Envisioning and Planning) in self-reflection and goal-setting aimed at discovering *what matters most* (WMM) and charting a course for change and progress. The first step (Envisioning) is to develop an image of your ideal future, identifying what matters most to you as well as brainstorming possible ways to better align each aspect of your life with what you care most about. The second step is to develop a Life Plan and publish it in a one-page, time-based format. This plan will be your playbook and accountability tool that will be updated for your monthly and annual targets along your journey.

My friend, Andy Bailey, an executive coach and the author of *No Try, Only Do*, has created a set of tools that we have adapted with his permission for the planning part of the LOS. The Planning process is built around seven areas; Family, Finance, Faith, Fitness, Friends, Fun, and Field.

We have found that the initial process of going through the two steps, envisioning and planning, can be more fruitful if you carve out some time and go someplace for a personal one- or two-day retreat. Even better would be to do this with your spouse or life partner. Will Verity coined the term "Weekend in the Woods" for the experience he and his wife Paula had working through such questions. At a minimum you will have to enlist the support of a trusted friend to serve as your accountability coach and sounding board. The odds of your success skyrocket when you declare your intention to others, out loud and on paper. The process of communicating anchors the work in the universe and brings focus and accountability.

> **The odds of your success skyrocket when you declare your intention to others, out loud and on paper.**

Life is best understood backwards, but must be experienced forward. Looking back, I have experienced places described as *"thin places."* Places where the veil between heaven and earth is quite transparent. These are places where the divine and our world collapses and we can catch glimpses of transcendence and vision. These are the places for this kind of work. They are often found in the mountains and forests, around lakes and oceans. Where natural beauty surrounds.

Find a *thin place* like Will and Paula's cabin in the woods, a beach house, or a mountain retreat. Disconnect from your electronics, eliminate social media, and use philosophy and faith to ground yourself. Think clearly and freely. You can also add in some fun—bring some wine, games, or other activities to reward yourself for progress made. Take walks, notice nature and its amazing order, and envision how you can play in its symphony. No matter where you do it, make sure you pick a time when you can devote *all* of your attention—don't cram it in between other activities! Put the time on the calendar, get some color markers and big sticky notes, and set off. It is likely to be some of the most valuable time you spend this year.

Your Life Plan: Envisioning

We've established the benefits and importance of having a Purpose in life. Importantly, our Purpose must have context and a path to becoming true. We all seek a unifying *Purpose* that serves as a filter for all your intentional choices. Something like, "to serve others."

As you begin to reimagine life, a slight admonition might be in order. Remember we in America are living in the most prosperous times man has ever known. It affords us so many luxuries and opportunities for service. The most negative aspect of our prosperity is the self-centeredness it has bred in our culture. This self-centeredness is often manifested in entitlement, gluttonous behaviors, abdication of civil engagement, spiritual and religious lethargy, and, worst of all, greed. Remember you can chart a course to do well and do good. Keep these thoughts close as you establish your north star.

Like eating an elephant, we have to break the envisioning process down into smaller, more manageable bites. Here are the seven functional segments we want to work through—let's call them the *7 Fs*:

- **Family:** Spouses, partners, children, relatives, vacations, intimacy, parenting
- **Finance:** Cash flow, debt, net worth, wills, estate planning, philanthropy
- **Faith:** Morals/ethics, spiritual accountability, self-esteem, meditation, ministry, church
- **Fitness:** Physical/mental health, nutrition, stress management, healing, healthy living, exercise
- **Friends:** Friends, community, neighbors, social groups, workplace relations
- **Fun:** Sports, hobbies, travel, relaxation, avocations, entertainment
- **Field:** Profession, career progression, culture, professional development, peers, organizations

Will and Paula's weekend in the woods involved moving deeper through the layers of desire, reaching for more meaning. Using a couple of tablet boards and some wine, they came away with a new life plan that would send them to a new location and the beginnings of a new business.

In envisioning, you identify what matters most to you in each of the 7 Fs and flesh out possible ways to better act in accordance with this principle. You can explore your desires in terms outlined in Maslow's Hierarchy of Needs. If you find your answers are landing on levels 1 or 2, reconsider and see if you can push higher up the hierarchy reaching for levels 4 and 5. If now is not the time for such lofty pursuits, no worries. Sometimes we just have more immediate needs. This is not a one and done process. You will have future sessions to revisit these ideas.

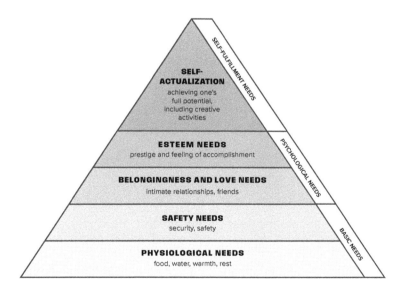

Your Fitness and Finances (think *health* and *wealth*) are the foundational aspects of your life, while Family, Friends, Fun, Field, and Faith are the building blocks. You have to build a strong foundation in order to be able to build a Purpose-driven, fulfilling life that you control. But we have found that the motivation to invest in your Fitness and your Finances is influenced by how compelling your vision is for the building blocks of your life. In other words, if you are excited about what you are doing, where you are doing it, and who you are doing it with, then you are more likely to be motivated to take care of yourself and make the financial investments needed to live your best life.

Our experience with this behavior completely supports the research on the health and aging benefits of the absolutely free commodity of *Purpose*. It seems counter-intuitive, but it's the way we are wired. If you care deeply about something, you want to put it in the strongest possible position for success. The data shows for instance that people may love their pets much more than they love themselves.[14] I'm sure you are saying, *Wait! Not true! You haven't met my crazy clients.* Did you know your clients are more likely to administer your prescription than they are to acquire and take their own prescribed medication? Go figure. Do we really have so much disdain for our own lives that we value them less than our pets?

We hope this process for taking control of your life gets you to fall deeply into commitment to yourself. If this is true, you naturally will take better care of your health and wealth.

---

14 BI Editorial. 2021. "When People Love Pets More Than Themselves—Business Insurance." Business Insurance. April 28, 2021. https://www.businessinsurance.com/when-people-love-pets-more-than-themselves-halifax-pet-insurance-yahoo-finance/.

Admittedly it's a bit of a hack on the psyche but the results are well worth it.

Envisioning Your Life Plan: Pen to Paper

Like any journey, we must begin with a clear knowledge of where we are now. So, let's get started with an assessment of our current state. Complete the following exercise to rank the seven areas of life. You may want to apply a little extra attention to the lower scoring categories as you move through the exercise.

YOUR LIFE PLAN ASSESSMENT

Where are you now...
For each of the 7 areas of your life, rate your level of satisfaction by scoring it 1-5 (1 = lowest level of satisfaction and 5 = highest level of satisfaction).

Family:	Spouse, Parents, Children, Extended Relatives, Vacations, Travel, Intimacy, Parenting Skills	1 2 3 4 5
Finance:	Taxes, Estate Planning, Wills, Career Development, Wealth Planning, Bookkeeping, Credit, Loans, Goals	1 2 3 4 5
Faith:	Morals/Ethics, Spiritual Accountability, Self-Esteem, Stewardship, Church/Ministry, Meditation	1 2 3 4 5
Fitness:	Physical Fitness, Nutrition, Stress Reduction, Medicine/Healing, Mind-Body Wellness, Healthy Living	1 2 3 4 5
Friends:	Friends, Community, Neighbors, Social Groups, Workplace Relations, Spiritual Community	1 2 3 4 5
Fun:	Sports, Hobbies, Travel, Relaxation, Events, Me-Time, Socialization, Entertainment	1 2 3 4 5
Field:	Profession, Forums, Salary, Career Progressions, Culture, Professional Development, Peers, Board Work, Committees	1 2 3 4 5

Next, for each of the seven components, we are going to ask you to narrow your focus to the *one* thing that is most important to you at this time in your life. Yes, these can and should change as you progress, and you will have to do this exercise a few times in life to manage the flow. I'm often asked how frequently one should revisit this process. The answer is unique to each person, and I usually recommend refreshing your overall plan when 30-40 percent of your long-term goals have been achieved, if your circumstances change materially, or upon the plan's maturity date.

Our hope is that you will get comfortable with the process we have laid out such that you can apply it to additional items over time to better align all aspects of your life with what matters most.

You may need more space than what's provided, so have some paper handy. For a printable version, or to check out a sample plan, please visit: www.theprosperousvet.com

1. YOUR LIFE PLAN: ENVISIONING FAMILY

Narrow your focus on what is most important to you at this time in your life. Make notes as you process through these prompts.

1. Family includes spouses, partners, children, extended family, parenting, vacations together. Sometimes it helps to just write down everything you can related to family and then prioritize them.

2. Pick the aspect of Family that is most important to you and write down what is working and what is not working – what needs improvement?? What would you like to do more of or less of in regard to this family component?

3. Describe your ideal vision of this part of Family.

4. Next write down all the possible ways you can think of to make this aspect of Family better align with your ideal vision. It is important that you let yourself go during this brainstorming exercise – don't judge whether the possibility is realistic – just get it down on paper.

2. YOUR LIFE PLAN: ENVISIONING FIELD

Narrow your focus on what is most important to you at this time in your life. Make notes as you process through these prompts.

---

1. Field is your profession and all that it encompasses. Continuing education, acquisition of new skills, organizations you participate in, etc. Also consider your career progression, colleagues, and workplace relations and even where you practice or the type of practice. Consider all the areas of your Field and write them down below.

---

2. Next identify what you care most about in each of these aspects of your Field. If for instance you determined that where you practice is the most important, consider how important is the weather, the culture, access to outdoor activities, proximity to the beach or to mountains, schools, work opportunities, etc. What aspects about the where you practice do you care most about and what would you like to change or improve?

---

3. Brainstorm all the possibilities you can think of to enhance, modify, or completely change about your professional activities. Don't limit your thinking. Remember, I switched from a life in investment banking and private equity to veterinary medicine.

---

4. Now look over your list of possibilities and create a vision for how you would like each "most important" aspect of your Field to look longer term? Be aspirational and make sure the vision you create in the future gives you energy in the present – if it does not move you then perhaps it is not aspirational enough?

3. YOUR LIFE PLAN: ENVISIONING FRIENDS & FUN

Narrow your focus on what is most important to you at this time in your life. Make notes as you process through these prompts.

1. Friends and Fun are all the people you spend your life with and how you spend your time away from work. Consider all these categories and list the one that really matter to you and then identify who matters most and what activities you engage in or want to engage it. Make note of any that really do not matter all that much.

2. Next create a list of all the possible ways you could enhance your relationship with those Friends you care most about. How could you spend more time with them? Are there some people you would like to spend less time with? Do you fit in with the culture in your workplace? Would you like to have more friends? If so, how might you meet them? Are there people you would like to spend less time with?

3. Next create a list of all the possible ways you could enhance your free time. Deepening of skills, expanding hobbies, more entertainment of a particular type. How could you spend more time with activities and including the friends that matter most? Are there some people you would like to spend less time with? Do you fit in with the culture in your workplace? Would you like to have more friends? If so, how might you meet them? Are there people you would like to spend less time with?

4. Now look over your list of possibilities and create a vision for how you would like each "most important" place to look longer term. Where do you want to spend your time? Be aspirational and make sure the vision you create in the future gives you energy in the present – if it does not move you then perhaps it is not aspirational enough?

4. YOUR LIFE PLAN: ENVISIONING FAITH & FITNESS

Narrow your focus on what is most important to you at this time in your life. Make notes as you process through these prompts.

1. Your Person includes your physical, emotional and spiritual health. Physical health means items such as weight, your level of fitness, any illnesses or diseases you might have, your energy level and your sleep. Emotional health includes your attitude and overall level of happiness, relationships, empathy, stress level and contentment. Your spiritual health relates to your system of believes about how the universe is organized and how you fit into the system. For many this is faith in God. Whatever you believe, it has be rock solid at least from your point of view. Now, list below which aspects of your Fitness and Faith are important to you and then make note of which aspects matter most.

2. Next brainstorm a list of all the possible ways you could enhance or improve the aspects of your Fitness and Faith that matter most to you?

3. Now look over your list of possibilities and create a vision for how you would like each "most important" of your Fitness and Faith to look at longer term. How much will you weigh? How much energy will you have? How happy will you be? How will develop your faith or belief system? Be aspirational and make sure the vision you create in the future gives you energy in the present – if it does not move you then perhaps it is not aspirational enough?

5. YOUR LIFE PLAN: ENVISIONING FINANCE

Narrow your focus on what is most important to you at this time in your life. Make notes as you process through these prompts.

1. Finance includes all aspects of your financial life including your level of income and expenses, your debt, savings, cash flow streams, assets, investments, your insurance coverage and your tax and estate planning. What is working well in each of these areas and what is not working?

2. Now brainstorm a list of possible ways that you could enhance or improve the areas that matter most to you. Would you like to spend less and save more? Own for cash flow streams? Would you like to change the way and/or amount you have invested?

3. Now look over your list of possibilities and create a vision for how you would like each "most important" aspect of your financial health to look longer term. How much passive income will you have? What will you be worth in financial terms? Will you have complete financial freedom? If so, by when? Be aspirational and make sure the vision you create in the future gives you energy in the present – if it does not move you then perhaps it is not aspirational enough?

Your Life Plan: Planning

Armed with the results of your Envisioning exercise, it is time to develop and publish a time-bound and measurable plan. Strategic planning happens every quarter in well-run organizations around the world. If you come from a business background, it is likely you have experienced some form of annual and quarterly planning. In fact, a whole consulting industry has grown up around organizational planning. Most of the best systems trace their roots back to foundational scholars like Peter Drucker or Jim Collins. These systems usually begin with discovering the Core Values and Purpose of an organization, and then using these as the unifying theme for the culture and activities of the organization.

In organizations, a planning process brings transparency and clarity to what a group of people are trying to accomplish. It also allows for resources to be focused on concrete results in the short-term and for creating paths for longer-term success. (This is how we believe we should run our practices—but I digress, as this is a topic for another book.) In our LOS planning process, there is really only one key consumer of your values and Purpose engine, you!

There are many authors and techniques available for businesses to approach strategic planning, but surprisingly fewer translations for individuals, who after all are the reasons those organizations succeed. It seems to us that if an organization's people had a better plan for their life, then they would contribute to their organizations at a higher level. One excellent example of prioritizing both people and organizations comes from Andy Bailey's work, where he integrates the plan for the organization with the health of the lives of its leaders.

One of my favorites of Jordan Peterson's 12 Rules is rule #4, which reads: *"Compare yourself to who you were yesterday, not to who someone else is today"* Simple enough? Not really. We live in a world that facilitates comparison at every turn. Facebook, Instagram, Pinterest, TikTok—please, stop!—we must turn it off and ask ourselves, "Where am I today? Based on my vision, what are the targets I have developed?"

Planning any journey requires we begin with one simple foundational fact; where am I right now. As you begin, focus on taking small steps and planning in actionable measurable increments. Remember the Atomic Habits truth about the impact of a 1 percent daily improvement. Each goal you set must have a deadline, it should be quite precise so that it can be measured, and please make sure they are applicable to what matters most. Use the concepts of "**A**ctionable, **D**eadline, **A**pplicable and **M**easurable." These characteristics form the acronym, **ADAM**. Keep applying the ADAM test to each target in your plan.

Weaving together what matters most in each of the *7 Fs* creates an excellent array of high value targets to move toward over the next 90 days, one year, 5 year and 10-year periods.

Planning Your Life Plan: Pen to Paper

In planning, you are going to use your envisioning answers to create a Life Plan. You can use the template in this book, or create your own. Using your results of Your Life Plan Assessment and your Envisioning answers, you can arrive at goals and targets in four areas:

- Relationships
- Achievements
- Rituals
- Wealth

YOUR LIFE PLAN

What will your life look like 10 years from now...
(Target Date: ___/___/___)

Think about your future on your selected date and describe the things that are true in each category below. Make sure they are detailed and follow the ADAM rules.

Relationships	Achievements	Rituals	Wealth
Love, Family, Fiends, Self	Significance, Winning, Impact	Faith, Discipline, Fitness	Finance, Legacy, Freedom

Note: This exercise is completed for a date at least ten years from now and repeated (ahead) for a date one year out. The 1-year target builds to the 10-year plan. Finally, you will translate the one-year target to what you have to accomplish this month and complete the monthly form.

It helps to close your eyes and project yourself forward to a time at the planning horizon. Think about yourself 10 years from today. What is your age, health, etc? Run through each of the *7 Fs*.

Then, as you look one year from now, you can make updates monthly during the year until you reach the one-year goals. Around the 11th month of your planning year, you can also take time out to reset the next year's targets, taking care to align your goals with your 10-year plan.

YOUR LIFE PLAN
What will your life look like 1 year from now...
(Target Date: ___/___/___)

Think about your future on your selected date and describe the things that are true in each category below. Make sure they are detailed and follow the ADAM rules.

Relationships	Achievements	Rituals	Wealth
Love, Family, Fiends, Self	Significance, Winning, Impact	Faith, Discipline, Fitness	Finance, Legacy, Freedom

YOUR LIFE PLAN

Your Month...
This month, I will complete these goals in alignment with my Year.

SUN	MON	TUE	WED	THU	FRI	SUN
☐	☐	☐	☐	☐	☐	☐
☐	☐	☐	☐	☐	☐	☐
☐	☐	☐	☐	☐	☐	☐
☐	☐	☐	☐	☐	☐	☐
☐	☐	☐	☐	☐	☐	☐

CONCLUSION

By Andy Anderson

Before we close our inquiry into becoming a prosperous veterinarian, I'd like to share one last story. I've found that when you're moving along a path with a clear destination, and the journey is characterized by very low friction, it often means you're on the right track. As Matthew McConaughey would say, these are "green lights." My first partnership with Fred Williams was a total green light experience from the get-go.

Fred and I were vet school classmates. We had a lot in common in vet school but were in different life stages. I was married and trying to figure out being a husband and father to my one-year-old son while Fred was fresh out of undergrad without too much to tie him down. (Fred would later marry Michelle, who would become our dear friend as well. Fred and I both "married up" in our choice of Kim and Michelle who were completely involved in starting our business and have as strong of a bond as Fred and I.) Fred and I unknowingly and without intention ended up competing for class rank. He was #1 and I was a close second.

Both interested in small animal surgery, we pursued internships and residencies at Missouri and Tennessee, respectively. We re-established our friendship as we were starting our practice careers in Houston and Dallas. Fred was working hard and had his first child, and we were very focused on applying our skills and building our lives.

We started discussing a partnership while preparing for our board exam to become board-certified small animal surgeons. This exam requires about four months of intense study—Fred was studying in Dallas, and I was in Houston. We shared materials, encouraged each other, and organically our partnership began to take shape during this period of intense intellectual effort.

An important starting point was identifying both distinct and overlapping skill sets within our partnership. Fred had no formal business acumen but had seen his father successfully run his own veterinary practice, which made it easier for him to grasp the potential for success. Clinically, we had overlapping and unique skills, which together made us a highly capable team. This diverse skill set allowed us to offer a tremendous service to our community when we combined our resources, equipment, facilities, and team.

We discussed the concept and considered both Austin and San Antonio as potential locations. We arranged "weekend getaway" meetings with Kim and Michelle in these cities to explore the possibilities and discuss the details, such as who would relocate first, whether we would both move at the same time, and how much capital we needed.

When it comes to partnerships, a major advantage is risk mitigation compared to doing something on your own. A co-creation approach allows you to bring together the best of two minds to sort out and make the best decisions. There is also the efficiency of combining resources; for instance, in our case, we brought together two families—Fred and Michelle, and Kim and myself—to start a business and figure everything out together. For risk-averse individuals or professions, partnerships lower the burden and risk, which can significantly accelerate the decision to proceed.

> **When it comes to partnerships, a major advantage is risk mitigation compared to doing something on your own. A co-creation approach allows you to bring together the best of two minds to sort out and make the best decisions.**

I started putting together the business plan, considering how we would acquire the necessary equipment and where we would lease our initial hospital. All of these discussions and plans were happening in the background as we prepared for the exam.

We then went to San Diego to take our exams, which was as gut-wrenching as you can imagine. We had decided that only one of us needed to pass, because the one who didn't pass could temporarily work under the other's certification until the next exam administration a year later. This way, we could still implement our business plan. After the exam, we had to wait about two months for the scores.

In the interim, I met a guy whose dog I had operated on. He was a human medical instrument sales rep, and I asked if he had any equipment for sale. He mentioned that he was retiring and had 25 years' worth of handheld surgical instruments and various OR equipment stored in his garage. I asked how much he wanted for all of it, and he said $10,000. This was incredible, as I had budgeted $150,000 for this equipment. I loaded it up in three Suburban loads, took it all home, and laid it out in a room. When Fred came down and saw it, he was nearly in tears seeing all the equipment we needed for only $10,000. This was a major green light in our partnership development. We were really moving now.

We also found an emergency clinic owned by shareholders who were willing to lease us space at an affordable price. The synergy of our relationship continued to yield exceptional outcomes for our families, our practice, our patients, our clients, and our employees. We were able to live by the principles of authenticity and Purpose discussed in the book, benefiting many people's lives while doing well financially.

The major green light for us to expand to a larger hospital and other locations was when we began to see that our approach was attracting other like-minded veterinarians and staff. There were not enough facilities or businesses doing what we did. We had other veterinarians we wanted to bring into the partnership, and they were eager to join, willing to take the risk and do the work.

We expanded to another city with our partner Justin Payne who began his career with us. Justin was a great veterinarian and "go getter" who quickly replicated our early success in another market. Justin's wife Nicol likewise partnered with Kim and Michelle and played an important role in the administration of the practice. Justin used the principles laid out in this book to invest and build prosperity and freedom.

Whenever the right opportunity with the right veterinarian came together, it was an easy decision to move forward. We had the capital and essentially have been applying the same model we started with to new partners. By approaching expansion as a partnership, we could continue to grow by expanding our circle of prosperity.

> **By approaching expansion as a partnership, we could continue to grow by expanding our circle of prosperity.**

And that's what it's all about. Frank Hevrdejs once told me, "*Everyone* has opportunities cross their paths. Whether they take form in business, service, or personal development, the outcomes are a result of choices made to pursue the available opportunities." Many people just get stuck and can't say 'yes' to the opportunities they are given.

Nothing we have presented here is out of your reach. We have provided you a playbook of sorts and an approach to execution. Our hope is these concepts now feel approachable and that you will choose to take control of your life and become prosperous and more joyful through their application.

We wish for you great success and are cheering you on while you advance and transform our esteemed profession. Be a force for principled leadership and encouragement in your communities, practices, faith, and families! Above all else make sure to share your wisdom, gratitude, and prosperity with others.

**For more information,
please visit https://theprosperousvet.com or contact
info@theprosperousvet.com**

ACKNOWLEDGMENTS

Undertaking to write *The Prosperous Veterinarian* was ultimately a team effort. To my contributing authors, I offer my gratitude for believing in the project and the good that might come from our collective efforts. Included in this group is Eland Mann, who brought years of editing experience and a sense of readability to our project.

To all those who shared freely of their experiences and the stories of their journeys so that I could pay their knowledge forward, thank you. Mentorship is fundamental to our profession, and your contributions support that tradition in a beautiful way. Among my most important mentors are Steve Taylor, DVM, DACVIM; Sandy Seamans, DVM; Frank Hevrdejs; Gordon Cain; John Payne, DVM, DACVS; Jim Tomlinson, DVM, DACVS; and Bill Daly, DVM, DACVS.

I have been blessed to have many great partners in business and life. In appreciation I call out particularly Fred Williams, DVM, DACVS, Will Verity, Bob Grusky, Shawn McLallen, and Vaughn Brock, each of whom have been steadfast in providing support and wise counsel over decades. Additionally, they have been among my closest and enduring friends. Also, thank you to Andy Bailey for his teaching and contributions, and for allowing his materials to be adapted for our Life Operating System (www.Boundless.me).

Lastly, my acknowledgements would be incomplete without the Rev. William Patrick Gahan. I stand in gratitude for his friendship and spiritual mentorship as well as his inciteful comments on the manuscript.

Most importantly, for the hours of discussion, editing, and honest feedback, to my wife and soulmate of thirty-seven years, Kim. I can only say I love you and thank you for believing in the crazy journey we are living.

ABOUT THE AUTHOR

Dr. Andy Anderson, DVM, MBA, traces his roots to Houston, Texas, where he encountered a wonderful veterinarian named Dr. Bruce Ueckert. Bruce introduced Andy's thirteen-year-old curious mind to the wonders of veterinary medicine.

Throughout Andy's education at Texas A&M University and Harvard Business School, and later during his surgical residency at the University of Missouri, his appreciation for the role veterinarians play in their communities was ever-present. This led him to serve in leadership positions in the American College of Veterinary Surgeons and in organizations changing the landscape of veterinary medicine.

Now in his sixties, Andy splits his time between the Texas Hill Country and Colorado. He enjoys hiking, ranching, fly-fishing, golf, and snow skiing. With his wife of thirty-seven years, Kim, the Andersons are enjoying their grandsons, George and Spencer Anderson, along with their son, Chase, and his wife, Elizabeth. Dr. Anderson serves on several non-profit boards including the Texas Biomedical Research Institute. The Andersons attend Christ Episcopal Church.